Third Drawer from the Top

This script is published by
DCG Publications.

All inquiries regarding purchase of further scripts and current royalty rates should be addressed to:

DCG Media Group
Vamos 73008
Chania
Crete
Greece

Email: info@dcgmediagroup.com
www.dcgmediagroup.com

Conditions

- ❖ All DCG Publications scripts are fully protected by the copyright acts. Under no circumstances must they be reproduced by photo-copying or any other means, either in whole or in part.

- ❖ The license to perform referred to above only relates to live performances of this script. A separate license is required for video-taping or sound recording, which will be issued on receipt of the appropriate fee.

- ❖ The name of the author shall be clearly stated on all publicity, programs etc. The program credits shall state "Script provided by DCG Publications".

Third Drawer from the Top

By

Glyn Idris Jones

DCG
Publications

First Published in Greece 2011

© Glyn Idris Jones
The author's moral rights have been asserted

Douglas Foote
DCG Publications
www.dcgmediagroup.com

ISBN 978-960-9610-01-8

Typeset by
DCG Publications

For
Tom Arthur

with thanks
for the American experience

First Produced
as a play reading by the
National Theatre Fraternity
University of Alabama

7th February 2011

Advisor
David Harwell

Third Drawer from the Top

CAST -

JOSH

CINDY

DEEDEE

DONNY

MARK

KRISTEN

DR GARDNER

DOUGLAS (VOICE OFF)

> Note on the use of slang: As this play takes place in a college setting and, as all but two of the characters are college students, a great deal of slang has been used in the dialogue. But slang changes fast and there is no objection to changes being made to keep up with the latest expressions.

ACT ONE

An off-campus apartment in a small Mid-Western town. The apartment is in a purpose-built block and what is seen is the main room with, beyond it, a dining / kitchen area. Access to this area is through a wide opening in the dividing wall of the two sections so that most of the dining / kitchen area can be seen.

There is a front door from an outside corridor and, on the opposite side of the main room, an arch leads through to the rest of the apartment beyond which a small hall gives access to two bedrooms and the bathroom, none of which are seen, possibly just one of the doors.

The kitchen has fitted units, an electric cooker, fridge, and microwave. There is also a dining table and chairs. Hidden behind one section of wall between main room and kitchen is a small table on which is a telephone, the cord of which can stretch to any part of the two rooms.

The furniture is Sears. There is a set of shelves on which are a few books, CD's, a television set, stereo system and a portable radio player in lurid colours - yellow and pink? Green and purple?

There are a few pathetic indoor plants, and the room is littered with empty soda and beer cans, plastic beakers, and ashtrays filled to overflowing. A few grubby garments, the odd shoe, notebooks and papers are scattered around.

It is late evening, a Saturday in early March. The

room is lit only by a streetlight filtering in through the windows in the fourth wall. From the apartment below there comes the muffled but loud enough to be irritating sound of a television set turned up very loud.*

The front door is flung open and CINDY enters, switching on the main light. She is followed by JOSH carrying a suitcase and with a tote bag slung over his shoulder. They wear winter over clothes.

CINDY: This is it. (*She takes in the debris.*) Oh, shit! I do not believe it. I do not believe it! (*She slams the door behind JOSH.*) I told those guys. I told them! I spent three days cleaning up this place especially for you. Look at it! Look at this! (*She picks up an ashtray, spills some of the contents, and puts it down.*) This way. (*She crosses towards the arch leading to the bedrooms.*) Well it's not Mark this time. He's gone home for the weekend. But Donny's staying here because he got thrown out of his own apartment and he's obviously had them in.

The telephone rings. CINDY, taking off her cap and scarf as she goes, changes direction and heads for the phone. JOSH, who has already put down his suitcase once, now puts it down again, but CINDY points the way to the bedroom.

Just go through there, to the left.

JOSH does so. CINDY picks up the phone.

Yo!

Deedee's voice is heard on the other end.

DEEDEE: Hi, Cindy! I tried to get you on your cell but it's switched off. I know this may actually seem like a silly question because I know he doesn't actually live there but is Donny in?

CINDY: Actually, no.

DEEDEE: Is this Cindy?

CINDY: No, it's (*name of current 1st Lady*). She always answers the phone in this apartment.

DEEDEE: Hi, Cindy! This is Deedee.

CINDY: I know who it is, Deedee. You have a very distinctive voice. How would I describe it? Like a chipmunk in season.

DEEDEE: You never heard that!

CINDY: No, but I can imagine.

DEEDEE: Do you know where Donny is?

JOSH has returned and stands listening. He has removed his overcoat, scarf, etc.

CINDY: No, Deedee, I do not know where Donny is. I've just got back from the airport.

DEEDEE: The airport!

CINDY: (*Pulls the phone away from her ear then puts it back.*) Yes, Deedee. You know, that place where big silver birds go vroom vroom.

DEEDEE: Oh, you went to meet Josh. How is he? When am I going to meet him? This fabulous guy I've heard so much about.

CINDY: And when I do see Donny I'm going to kill him.

DEEDEE: Oh? Why?

CINDY: So tell him so from me.

DEEDEE: Yes, but why, Cindy?

CINDY: Because... hold on...

Josh has been making signs. CINDY puts her hand over the mouthpiece.

JOSH: Bathroom.

CINDY: (*Indicating.*) That way.

JOSH: Thank you.

He disappears through the arch.

CINDY: (*Into phone.*) Because this place has been left looking like a landfill when I distinctly asked for it not to be, especially after it took me THREE FUCKING DAYS to CLEAN IT UP! That's why and goodbye!

She slams down the phone, stands fuming for a moment, looking round. She picks up a sweatshirt, regards it with distaste, throws it into another part of the room, kicks a shoe into a corner, crosses over to the shelves, selects a CD, slips it into the player. Two bars of rock and she presses the stop. She switches on the TV, presses every channel selector in quick succession, and switches it off. JOSH returns. CINDY moves away to look out of the window. He moves up behind and puts his arm around her. She does not move away but neither does she show any sign of response.

CINDY: Do you like my plants?

JOSH: Very nice. (*He kisses her neck.*)

CINDY: You should. They're all that's left of the hundreds I bought.

JOSH: What happened to the rest?

CINDY: I killed them with my black thumb. Each of those plants survived by losing a dozen brothers and sisters. Which makes them very expensive plants.

JOSH: Maybe you killed them with kindness.

CINDY: Nope. Black thumb. (*She holds up the thumb to show him, looks around the apartment.*) Look at this place. It's not for real.

JOSH: Cindy, I really don't mind what the place looks like. I'm not into surveying real estate. I came here to see you.

CINDY: It's truly weird, you know? Coming into an empty apartment like this. Usually it's like the Rose Bowl, it's like there are a million people in here. Even if it's only two and the cat it still feels like a million. And I like that. Don't you? This is really weird. And so quiet.

JOSH: This? ...is what you call quiet?

CINDY: Isn't it?

JOSH: Listen.

CINDY: (*Listens, and then.*) I don't hear anything.

JOSH: I knew it. We're breeding a generation of deaf children.

CINDY: What're you talking about? Are we going to stand here like this all evening?

JOSH: You don't like standing like this?

CINDY: (*Ducking out of his arms and heading for the phone table.*) Any messages? (*She looks at the answer phone.*) Hundreds. (*Heads for the fridge, at the same time casually examining her cell phone in one hand.*) Wanna drink? Beer maybe? (*She opens the fridge.*) No beer. Jeez, there's nothing but leftovers in this fridge. But no leftover beer. They've drunk it all. I'm going to kill whoever's responsible for this.

JOSH: With your black thumb?

CINDY: What's this? (*She opens a package, sniffs the contents.*) Mummified cheese... I think. Could be mummified anything. You know something? I think this is the very first piece of Monterey Jack I bought when I moved into the apartment. (*She tosses it across the kitchen, obviously towards the trash can behind the wall. There is a crash. She turns back to the fridge.*) A box of Girl Scout cookies. (*She opens the box.*) Correction. A box of one Girl Scout cookie. Split it with you?

JOSH shakes his head.

There's soda.

JOSH: Really, Cindy, I'm fine. I don't need anything. Not food-wise anyway.

CINDY: (*Puts away the phone, moves to the table, tossing away the cookie as she goes.*) Cigarettes... cigarettes... (*She picks up a pack. It's empty so she screws it up, drops it, picks up another, also empty. And another. Empty.*)

JOSH: (*Holding out his own.*) Here...

CINDY: Thanks.

He lights her cigarette and, using the opportunity of having her close to him, tries to take her in his arms again. The telephone rings. She uses this as an excuse to extricate herself, lifts the receiver and puts it down again.

We smoke too much in this apartment. Ninety percent of North America has given up this pollution of other people's airspace and we're making up the difference to keep the tobacco industry alive. We're heroes in North Carolina, you know that? If North Carolina were Cuba we'd be heroes of industry, first class. One day our lungs will go into a museum.

JOSH: Give it up.

CINDY: Give it up yourself.

JOSH: Too old. Habit's too ingrained.

CINDY: What do you mean anyway, give it up? I'm going to smoke myself to death and then my offspring can sue the tobacco company for billions of

	dollars and live happily ever after.
JOSH:	You're going to have offspring?
CINDY:	Oh, sure. They're gonna spring right outa me, by the dozen. I'm a breeder. They're gonna pop out like champagne corks.
JOSH:	Champagne corks don't pop out that easily.
CINDY:	What do you mean we're breeding a generation of deaf children?
JOSH:	You really don't hear anything?
CINDY:	What am I supposed to hear?
JOSH:	(*Pointing to the floor.*) That... That!
CINDY:	Oh, the television. We're used to that. Don't hear it anymore. It's the old lady in the apartment downstairs. She's deaf. She's old. She always plays it that loud. Sometimes till two, three in the morning. We ignore it. She's Jewish.

The telephone rings. She picks it up.

Yeh?

| DEEDEE: | Cindy, this is Deedee again. Can I come over and wait for Donny? |
| CINDY: | No, Deedee, you cannot come over and wait for Donny. |

She puts down the phone.

| JOSH: | Donny is your room-mate? |

CINDY: No. I told you, Mark is my room-mate, and his girlfriend is Kristen. Donny... why don't you sit down, Josh?... got thrown out of his apartment, together with HIS room mates, because they painted the walls.

JOSH: (*Sitting.*) So they painted the walls.

CINDY: Avocado, black and silver, with an aubergine ceiling.

JOSH: Sounds contemporary.

CINDY: Sounds graffiti. When I say they painted it, what I should of said was, they threw cans of paint in the general direction of whichever wall was nearest. I think they were stoned at the time. The results would indicate they were stoned.

JOSH: Psychedelic you might say.

CINDY: Might I?

JOSH: No, not really. It all sounds pretty old-fashioned. Sixties even. A lot of people made a lot of money in the sixties by throwing around cans of paint and calling it art. Made international reputations out of it. Museums and galleries are loaded with the stuff. Paid small fortunes for it because some dickhead called it art. Since then it's got even more Emperor's new clothes. Dead meat and dirty underwear. Anything goes.

CINDY: I take it you don't like modern art.

JOSH: I don't like trash that gives trash a bad name. To misquote a once great man, "Never has so much been paid by so many for so little."

CINDY: Who said that?

JOSH: Winston Churchill said something like that.

CINDY: Oh! What does it mean?

JOSH: Skip it.

CINDY: It means skip it?

JOSH: (*Laughing.*) We were getting close there.

CINDY: Tension's in the air. That happens.

JOSH: What happens?

CINDY: People get tense. Anyway, they were told to pack up and head on out.

JOSH: They?

CINDY: Donny and friends. They've been fined two hundred and eighty dollars which goes towards the cost of cleaning the room.

JOSH: Sounds reasonable.

CINDY: So Donny said, if he cleaned it up, would they get off with the fine? And the answer was no, a big fat no. So he went out and got two more cans of paint and wrote obscenities, I mean, OBSCENITIES you would not believe, all over the avocado, black and silver.

JOSH: What colour obscenities?

CINDY: Virgin white.

JOSH: Sounds ironic.

CINDY: The place looks like the way a New York subway used to look.

JOSH: So when are we going to New York? You don't even know what a New York subway looks like, or looked like.

CINDY: I've seen pictures.

JOSH: You keep putting it off. You want to go but keep putting it off.

CINDY: We've got to find the right time.

JOSH: We've got five days. Let's go now. Call the airport.

CINDY: Josh, it's your spring break, not mine. Mine isn't till next week. I can't help it if our college calendars don't coincide.

JOSH: Take the week off.

CINDY: You've got to be kidding! Do you know how much work I've got to get through? I'm not going to be great company this week as it is. But it's wonderful to see you, Josh. It truly is. I'm glad you came.

JOSH: Are you?

CINDY: Of course I am. I've told everybody about you. I never stop talking about you. Everyone's simply dying to meet you. And I've really missed you.

JOSH: Come here.

CINDY: I want a cup of coffee. You want some coffee? (*She goes into the kitchen and starts to make coffee.*) So Donny is staying here till he finds another place. And right now he isn't getting on too well with his ex-room-mates anyhow.

JOSH: Why's that?

He picks up a magazine from a side table and casually thumbs through it.

CINDY: I didn't ask, okay? If I don't ask and they don't tell me, I don't know about it, okay? It's got to be something to do with a check.

JOSH: Why's that?

CINDY: Donny writes out checks like every bank in the country is handing them out with his name on them. Look. (*She picks up a check wallet from a table and opens it.*) See? Not one left. (*She drops the book and stands looking at the ashtray on the table.*) I'd empty this ashtray only I think it's too heavy.

JOSH: Here, I'll do it.

CINDY: Sit down, Josh, it was a joke.

She empties the ashtray in the trash can, puts it back on the table, carries on with the coffee.

CINDY: So why are we breeding a generation of deaf children?

JOSH: It doesn't matter.

CINDY: Sure it does. I've got better things to do with my hands than learn to sign.

JOSH: Really? (*He lowers the magazine.*) I wish I could believe that.

CINDY: (*Sigh.*) Oh, Josh...

JOSH: Oh, Josh, what?

CINDY: It isn't possible.

JOSH: What do you mean, isn't possible?

CINDY: The apartment might be empty right this minute but in two minutes it could be like a football stadium in here. Shit, you never know who's coming in and who's going out. And I mean like that goes on about twenty-four hours a day.

JOSH: Does it matter?

CINDY: Of course it matters.

JOSH: You mean it's a question of decorum.

She looks at him, seems about to say something, thinks better of it, opens a cupboard door and takes out a mug.

JOSH: We have a bedroom.

CINDY: Correction. YOU have a bedroom. You have MY bedroom.

JOSH: What!

CINDY: Well of course you do. You'll have to excuse the cat litter tray.

JOSH: I don't believe this.

CINDY: It's the only place in the apartment to put it.

JOSH: I'm not talking about the fucking cat box!

CINDY: You sure you don't want a cup of coffee?

JOSH: Cindy!

CINDY: What?

JOSH: Where are you going to sleep?

She points to the floor.

Are you serious?

CINDY: As serious as a heart attack.

JOSH: I'm the one who's going to have the heart attack. You mean I flew six hours, three airplanes, to be with you for a few days, and I have to fly six hours, three airplanes back, and I hate airplanes, and you can't smoke in them anymore, to have you sleeping on the floor? In your own apartment? Because I'm in your bed? Where you should be?

CINDY: You seem to be making a very big deal out of it.

JOSH: It's a very big bed!

CINDY: I'm sorry, but that's how it is. I don't like sleeping with anyone anyway. It gets too hot.

JOSH: It's freezing. There's six inches of snow outside and it's minus twenty degrees in case you hadn't noticed.

CINDY: That's outside. And I sweat under the blankets at minus forty. And I feel too constricted sleeping with somebody.

JOSH: That's how lovers are supposed to sleep.

CINDY: We're not lovers, Josh.

JOSH: You keep telling me you love me. All your letters...

CINDY: I do! I think about you all the time. I miss you all the time. I talk about you all the time! You're a truly wonderful person and I love you.

JOSH: Then I don't ....

CINDY: (*Holding up her hand.*) Josh... this is making me uncomfortable.

JOSH: Oh, God forbid I should make you uncomfortable.

CINDY: (*Suddenly icy.*) I don't want to discuss it right now, okay?

JOSH: No, Cindy, it's not okay.

CINDY: You just got here, Josh. Give it a rest.

JOSH: I see, it's the old generation gap again, huh?

CINDY: You still haven't told me about my generation

being deaf.

JOSH: Are you asking about the heart or the ears?

CINDY: As far as I know there is nothing wrong with my heart and I have perfect hearing.

JOSH: Then how come you listen to what I say and not what I mean?

CINDY: Maybe because I'm just not ready to cope with what you mean so I don't want to hear it, okay?

JOSH: Cindy, it's been three years.

The phones rings. CINDY picks it up.

DEEDEE: Hi, Cindy! Listen can I come over and use your word processor? I really have to get this paper in and...

CINDY: Sure you can use my word processor, Deedee, but not right now, okay? Like try again in twenty-four hours. (*She slams down the phone.*) Boy, that girl never gives up. She'll ask if she can feed the cat next.

JOSH: Don't mock her devotion. It's a refreshing change.

CINDY: Bullshit! It'll be over in a week. They won't be able to stand the sight of each other. Speak of the devil.

Donny has appeared from the bedroom. He looks as though he is wearing an Afro wig, though it could be his real hair. His hands are thrust deep in the pockets of what looks like a World War I trench coat and two thirds of his legs are encased in baggy cut-offs. One sock is yellow, the other blue, and on his feet he has boat sized high-tops, one red and one green. He is yawning mightily. Donny obviously feels this is a way to show you are Bohemian, a serious artiste. On the other hand it's just because he puts on whatever's to hand.

DONNY: What time is it?

CINDY: Does it matter?

DONNY: I've been asleep. But I kept on hearing buzzing noises.

CINDY: That was the telephone, Donny. Why didn't you answer it?

DONNY: (*Yawn.*) Cause I was asleep. Hi! (*He waves a finger towards JOSH.*) Guess you must be the awesome Josh, huh?

JOSH: Awesome?

DONNY: (*Extending his hand which JOSH takes.*) Oh, truly awesome. (*He turns away and schlepps towards the kitchen and the phone.*) According to Cindy one of the most awesome men on planet Earth. (*He lifts the receiver, jabs at some numbers, yawns.*)

CINDY: I could kill you, Donny, you know that?

DONNY: Why, Cindy? (*He gropes inside an empty cigarette pack.*)

The phone is answered.

VOICE: Pete's Pizzeria. We make deep pan like no one else can.

JOSH goes back to his magazine.

DONNY: Yeh, I'd like a... (*Big yawn.*) ...Heparoooonie.

VOICE: Would you mind repeating that order please, sir?

DONNY: (*The yawn finished.*) An extra-large pepperoni and a side order of fries. (*To the others.*) You guys want some pizza? I can order two.

JOSH: (*Looks up, shakes his head.*) We've eaten already.

CINDY: At Luigi's.

DONNY: Only the best for my girl. (*Back to phone.*) Okay, 4179 Greenwood, numero ten. And a large coke. Will you take a check?

VOICE: And a large coke. Sorry, sir, no checks.

DONNY: Hold on. Either you guys got any cash?

JOSH looks up from his magazine and nods.

(*Into phone.*) Okay, cash it will be. (*He puts down the phone, turns to JOSH.*) I'll give you a check, okay?

CINDY: No, Donny, it is definitely not okay.

JOSH: It's okay.

CINDY: It is NOT! I repeat, NOT okay.

DONNY: Why isn't it okay, Cindy? I'll give the man a check, okay?

CINDY: There's not a check left in your check book, okay?

DONNY: I got plenty of books.

CINDY: And there's not a cent left in your checking account, okay? And apart from your room how many parking fines do you still have to pay?

JOSH: It's all right, Cindy, I really don't mind paying for Donny's pizza.

DONNY: She's right, you are truly amazing. I'm really most gratified to make your acquaintance, sir.

CINDY: (*To JOSH.*) Theatre speak. (*To DONNY.*) You see an upcoming week of endless pizza deliveries do you?

DONNY: You are fierce tonight, girl.

CINDY: Don-nee!!!

DONNY: (*To JOSH.*) You got a cigarette?

JOSH: Here...

DONNY: Oh, thanks.

CINDY: Don-neeeee!

DONNY: Yeah?

CINDY: Oh, forget it.

DONNY:	What's the matter with you, Cindy? Why you so stressed out, woman? You've done nothing for days but talk about Josh coming to visit, now you're all stressed out. Cool it.
CINDY:	Oh, go and call your stupid girlfriend.
DONNY:	(*Whistles - looks from one to the other.*) You two had a spat already? (*Attempt at a joke.*) I wondered why it was so hot in here.
CINDY:	It's hot in here, Donny, because the temperature outside is minus minus and the central heating in here is on plus plus and you're dressed for minus minus not plus plus. Don't tell me you've been sleeping in all that.
DONNY:	(*Looking down at his coat.*) Oh...yeah.
CINDY:	You really gross me out, Donny, you know that?

DONNY slips out of his coat which lands in a pile at his feet. He is wearing a Pete's Parlour T-shirt, or any other pizza parlour t-shirt, very grubby.

CINDY:	(*Groaning.*) Oh, God...Donny...
DONNY:	What?

CINDY points to the floor. DONNY looks down.

DONNY:	Oh Yeah. (*He picks up the coat and tosses it onto a chair.*)
CINDY:	Donny...
DONNY:	Now what?

She points to the coat. He picks it up again and marches with it towards the bedrooms.

You're really losing your shit, Cindy, You know that? Why you giving me this grief, girl?

And he disappears. CINDY groans loudly and sinks into the chair from which DONNY removed his coat. Silence as JOSH regards her and as they both obviously wait for DONNY to return. He doesn't.

JOSH: It's at moments like these that this awesome man you've been talking about for weeks would like to take you in his arms. But, presumably, that's against house rules, huh?

CINDY: (*Getting up.*) Excuse me, It's my turn to use the bathroom. (*She starts to go. Stops.*) You shouldn't have offered to pay for his pizza.

JOSH: Why not? I can't afford to buy someone a pizza?

CINDY: That's not the point. You're contributing to his early demise.

JOSH: How so?

CINDY: You've heard of death by chocolate? With this one it's death by pizza pig-out. What a slob. (*Goes. Stops.*) Now you know how he got his nickname.

JOSH: No, I don't know how he got his nickname. I don't even know what his nickname is.

CINDY: Smeg.

JOSH: Smeg?

CINDY: Think about it.

She disappears. JOSH looks around the apartment, picks up an ashtray, heads for the trash can. Half way there he stops.

JOSH: Ooooh, Smeg! Good grief! (*And he laughs, carries on and empties the ashtray, returns to the main area and notices a large garden ornament Buddha on the floor. He stops in front of it*) And what are you smiling at? I wouldn't have thought in this land of almost universal circumcision they'd even know the word, let alone the biological details. (*He puts down the ashtray, looks around the room.*) Well... looks like it's just you an' me, ole Buddha buddy. What're we gonna talk about? The human condition? One particular human condition, huh? Mine. Pathetic, isn't it? And what is it, you ask? I really wish I knew ole buddy, I wish you could tell me... What's that? Oooh, is that what it is? Of course, I should have realised. The male menopause, huh? So what am I doing? Making a last desperate grab at a gone forever youth? Anyway, how would you know about such things? You were above them, beyond all that, sitting under your sacred tree, contemplating your navel and attaining enlightenment. Would I attain enlightenment if I contemplated your navel? I've tried contemplating my own. All it does is make me horny. Sad, isn't it?

DONNY: What's sad?

He has appeared just in time to hear JOSH's last words. JOSH is a little embarrassed at being caught out talking to himself.

JOSH: Oh... I was... er... philosophising.

DONNY: (*Looks at the Buddha, looks at JOSH.*) Yeh, he has that effect on you sometimes. Good old, Buddha, baby. (*He gives the figure an affectionate pat on the head.*) We lifted him from somebody's yard. Gave him to Cindy as a present. I called Deedee, she's coming over.

JOSH: That's nice.

DONNY: Oh, sorry! Was that a mistake?

JOSH: What?

DONNY: I mean... you... and Cindy.

JOSH: Don't be silly. No mistake.

DONNY: We don't want to be in the way.

JOSH: Nobody's going to be in the way. If anybody's in the way, I am. You live here after all.

DONNY: No, I don't live here. This is temporary sanctuary. (*He goes into an imitation of Charles Laughton.*) "Sanctuary! Sanctuary! Hahaha, sanctuary!" Did you ever see that movie? "The Hunchback of Notre Dame?"

JOSH nods.

Wasn't Laughton amazing? (*He kneels, leaning forward with his hands behind his back as though tied.*) "Water... water... water..." (*Then he looks up to see Esmerelda offering him water, turns his head away, looks up again, shyly, opens his twisted mouth, tongue hanging out, plays the scene for all its worth.*) Wasn't that an amazing scene? Very symbolic. Beauty offering the beast the water of life. Love.

JOSH: Pity.

DONNY: Love.

JOSH: (*Shrugs.*) If you say so.

DONNY: (*Squatting cross-legged on the floor.*) It's the same kind of sexual symbolism like at the end of "The Grapes Of Wrath" when the girl offers the old man milk from her breast.

JOSH: Hope.

DONNY: Love.

JOSH: If you say so.

DONNY: All right, we'll agree to disagree.

JOSH: Sounds like a good compromise.

DONNY: Only temporary. I don't like compromise.

JOSH: Youth never does.

DONNY: (*Deciding to change the subject.*) How goes it with your l'il ole Southern university then?

JOSH: Mah l'il ole Southern university is Southern but it ain't that ole an' it ain't that l'il an' it's thriving mightily, thank you kineley.

DONNY: You're history, huh?

JOSH: Ancient.

DONNY: That's your period?

JOSH: No, my period is the Civil War.

DONNY: Oh. So you know all there is to know about ole Grant, and Lee, and Jackson, and the rest of them.

JOSH: No, Donny, I don't know all there is to know about them. It isn't possible to know ALL about anybody. It isn't possible to know about the living, about those closest and dearest to you. How is it possible to know all about the long since dead, who existed in other people's minds, who come to you through other people's words? What's your major?

DONNY: Theatre.

JOSH: Oh of course. So you know all about Shakespeare?

DONNY: I WAS speaking figuratively.

JOSH: I know.

DONNY: Making conversation.

JOSH: I'm sorry.

DONNY: (*Getting up.*) I tell you what, I'll go over to Deedee's.

JOSH: Look, there's really no need.

But DONNY is already on his way to the bedroom to

fetch his coat.

What about your pizza?

DONNY: You can take care of the man and Cindy can call me. Deedee's only two minutes down the block.

He has gone.

JOSH: Now why did I do that? (*To the Buddha.*) I have an acute sense of impending disaster here.

DONNY returns, putting on his coat, crosses the room to the front door, opens it...

DONNY: See you later. (*And goes out*).

JOSH: Shee-it!

SCENE TWO - SUNDAY EVENING

DONNY is pacing the kitchen area, a slice of cold pizza in one hand, a book in the other. He is learning his lines. He makes a histrionic gesture and the pizza flies out of his hand to land on the floor. He takes another slice from the open box on the table and carries on.

There is a wail from the bedroom followed by a despairing cry.

DEEDEE: Don-nee!

DONNY belches loudly takes another bite at the pizza.

Oh, SHIT! (*Silence.*) Don-neeeeee!

DONNY: Now what's the problem?

DEEDEE: I've lost it!

DONNY: You lost it a long time ago, girl.

DEEDEE: I can't get it back! I can't find it!

DEEDEE appears in the arch. She is a stunner in an "ALL-American girl" kinda way, and DEEDEE believes in showing herself off to maximum advantage.

I've lost it, Donny.

DONNY: No way. If you didn't instruct the computer to trash it, it's in there someplace.

DEEDEE: I don't believe it. (*She waves an arm towards the windows.*) It's out there in the wild blue yonder. It's heading fast on its way to Uranus or floating around in outer space.

DONNY: The only thing that's floating around in outer space is what passes for your mind, bubblehead.

DEEDEE: Oh, is that so? You have such an oversized left brain of course.

DONNY: Double bubblehead. So do you mind if I get on with my lines now? I've got rehearsal tomorrow and I'm supposed to be off the book.

DEEDEE: And if I don't get this paper finished for tomorrow I'm in the book, Doctor Gardner's big fat black book. So, please, Donny! Come and help. It won't take two seconds you are such a genius.

DONNY: Dee. (*Dramatic with gestured emphasis.*) I am trying to get my shit together here... with this French dude, Ionesco, and I am on the brink of a nervous burn-out. I do not understand theatre of the absurd.

DEEDEE: You're not meant to understand it. You're meant to feel it.

DONNY: (*Stares at her.*) Is that so?

DEEDEE: It's what modern art is all about, Donny. Feeling. Doesn't matter what you feel as long as you feel something. You can look at what someone calls a work of art and say, "That is but total SHIT" and that's okay because it probably is shit but at least you've reacted. You know the first time I truly appreciated the meaning of the absurd? When I auditioned for cheerleader.

DONNY: Okay. But I don't feel anything either and I gotta have some idea of what's the play's all about.

DEEDEE: It's all about rape.

DONNY: What?

DEEDEE: Of course it is. From what I've read of it that's perfectly obvious.

DONNY: Then how come it isn't obvious to me?

DEEDEE: You're not a woman.

DONNY: It's that obvious? Anyway, it can't be that, he doesn't touch her.

DEEDEE: Oh, he doesn't molest her physically. It's mental. Which is why it wasn't obvious to you.

DONNY: You mean it's all about mind-fucking?

DEEDEE: Isn't that what it's usually about.

DONNY: Deedee! You DO have a brain.

DEEDEE: Well of course I have. I wouldn't be at college if I hadn't.

DONNY: I wouldn't be too sure of that. I'll come and retrieve your paper from outer space. What's it about anyway?

DEEDEE: The historical accuracy of Shakespeare's Henry the Fourth, Part One.

DONNY: Whoa!

DEEDEE: I was thinking of doing a paper on Anouilh's Beckett and Sir Thomas More in "A Man For All Seasons" and how they achieve martyrdom in the relative plays... but I think I'll leave that for finals.

DONNY: (*Pizza suspended in mid-air.*) Well dip me in shit and candy me over! You ARE from outer space. You're a Vulcan. How come nobody ever guessed?

DEEDEE: Because there is still a great deal of prejudice against intelligent women and I don't believe in antagonising further an already highly nervous male animal.

She disappears into the bedroom leaving a dumbfounded DONNY, pizza slice in hand, to follow her. The front door opens and CINDY enters, followed by JOSH who pushes the door closed with his shoulders. They are both laden down with brown paper bags from the grocery and head for the kitchen. CINDY disappears to puts her bags down on a work top out of sight.

JOSH: Brrr! Je-SUS! It is cold! Would you believe it was in the sixties when I left hohohoooooo...!

He has stepped on Donny's discarded piece of pizza and goes crashing face first into the fridge door. CINDY reappears.

CINDY: Oh, my God! Are you all right?

JOSH turns to face her.

JOSH: Who had the bag with the eggs? (*He looks down into one of his bags.*) I have the bag with the eggs. Want an omelette?

CINDY: Here, give me those. (*She takes the bags and puts them down.*) Now what could... (*She picks up the remains of the pizza.*) I might have known. DON-NEEE!

JOSH eases himself away from the fridge door, lets out a yell, clutches his back, and falls back again.

JOSH: Ow!

CINDY: What's the matter? Are you hurt?

JOSH: I'm hurt.

CINDY: Here, let me help you. (*She takes his arm and leads him towards a chair.*) Sit down. Sit.

She holds his arm as he gingerly lowers himself into the chair.

JOSH: If it brings us this close I should get hurt more often.

CINDY: Quit it, Josh. DON-NEEE!

DONNY: (*Appearing.*) Yep?

CINDY: (*Pointing at JOSH.*) Look what you've done.

DONNY: What?

CINDY: You are a total pig, Donny Kellerman. And pigs live in pigsties, not apartments, except in this apartment where a pig happens to be living but not for long.

DONNY: Get off my case, girl. Just tell me what happened.

CINDY: (*Waving the remains of the pizza slice under his nose and then heading for the trash can to dump it.*) This happened! This! How you feeling, Josh?

JOSH: I'll live.

DONNY: Hey, I'm real sorry about this, man. Do you have insurance?

CINDY: Do you? He could sue you, you know that?

JOSH: It's okay, Donny, forget it. Accidents will happen.

CINDY: So will law suits.

DEEDEE appears.

JOSH: And I don't think there'll be any need for any hospitalization here.

DEEDEE: What happened?

CINDY: Donny Piggerman happened, that's what happened. (*To JOSH.*) Maybe you ought to lie down.

DONNY: Maybe he ought to go to the Health Centre.

CINDY: It's Sunday, Donny, in case you hadn't noticed. The Health Centre is closed. Students don't get sick over the week-end. They get sick Monday to Friday between the hours of nine and five.

DEEDEE: And anyway, if he went to the Health Centre, all they'd do is give him an aspirin.

CINDY: Oh, Josh, this is Deedee.

DEEDEE: Hi! (*She waggles her fingers.*)

JOSH: Hi! (*He waggles his, tries to get up, lets out a yelp, and subsides.*)

DEEDEE: They gave me an aspirin for my mono. If you were pregnant they'd give you an aspirin.

DONNY: Even the Health Centre would know he isn't pregnant.

DEEDEE: They'd still prescribe aspirin.

CINDY: Then why don't we just do that? There's a

                        medicine cabinet in the bathroom crammed with aspirin.

DEEDEE: We haven't diagnosed his symptoms.

CINDY: Since when was your major medical science?

DEEDEE: Aspirin could be the wrong thing.

CINDY: It's never the wrong thing.

DEEDEE: It is if he's got ulcers?

CINDY: What are your symptoms?

JOSH: Oh, talking to me? I thought you had excluded me from this medical council. Well, my symptoms seem to be fairly straightforward. Every time I move, the muscles in my lumbar region seem to go into spasm.

DEEDEE: Aspirin.

CINDY: Deedee!

DEEDEE: He's pulled a muscle. Possibly trapped a nerve. It's lumbago. Aspirin to ease the pain and a nice rub with Ben-gay to relax the muscle. Would you like me to do it for you?

           JOSH looks at DEEDEE, looks at CINDY.

JOSH: Thank you, I think I can rub in my own Ben-gay. Just let me get out of this chair.

ALL 3:   Here!

           They close in and help him to his feet, not without

some decidedly painful reactions from JOSH. CINDY holds one arm, DEEDEE the other.

CINDY: Okay?

JOSH: (*Nods.*) Yes, thank you. I can manage now.

Watched by the others he creaks his way towards the bathroom.

This is really embarrassing.

CINDY: Josh, your coat.

She takes his scarf and gloves, helps him off with his overcoat.

DEEDEE: And your jacket. Here...

She helps him off with the jacket, hands it to CINDY.

Easy does it. Don't want to go into spasm again, do we?

DONNY goes back to his pizza and his book. JOSH disappears towards the bathroom.

CINDY: You'll find the Ben-gay on the top shelf. I'll put these in the bedroom.

CINDY goes. DEEDEE moves towards the kitchen, folds her arms and stands surveying DONNY. He looks up from his book.

DEEDEE: Well?

DONNY: What?

DEEDEE: So what happened?

DONNY: Why ask me?

DEEDEE: Because it obviously had something to do with you.

DONNY: He slipped on a piece of pizza I forgot to pick up off the floor. Satisfied?

DEEDEE: Donny, sometimes you are so cute you could die of the cutes, you know that?

DONNY: Right on.

DEEDEE: But, as Cindy says, you are also a total pig.

DONNY: Well dip me in shit, Deedee, he should ha' watched where he was putting his feet.

DEEDEE: Pig. How come you can consume pizza by the megaton and you don't get porky?

DONNY: I have a high metabolic rate.

DEEDEE: A sloth has a high metabolic rate?

DONNY: Make up your mind, woman. I can't be a sloth AND a pig.

DEEDEE: Course you can. A cute piggish sloth. That about sums you up.

DONNY: Or a cute slothful pig. Anyway, talking about cute, you were getting pretty cutesy yourself there for a minute, nursie. "Would you like me to do it for you?" How come you just gotta flirt with every man you see?

DEEDEE: Instinct. I have a natural lovin' nature. And the man was in intense pain. It's that old time mothering thing.

DONNY: You can't have any kind of instinct for a man old enough to be your grandfather.

DEEDEE: Hmnnn... he does seem a bit old for her doesn't he?

DONNY: Yeh. I never figured on Cindy needing a father figure.

DEEDEE: It won't work.

DONNY: How come?

DEEDEE: Donny, there are some gaps in this world you can cross, like I've managed to do with you. But there are some you can't, and the generation gap is the Grand Canyon of them all, believe me. You can't even hang-glide over it. Give us a bite.

She leans forward and he holds out the pizza slice for her to take a bite.

Of course some girls ARE attracted to older men. There's a couple of horny professors in this outfit have laid a few students in their time. What attracts people to people?

DONNY: Or pigs to pigs?

DEEDEE: Opposites attract.

DONNY: Like opposite sexes.

DEEDEE: No, Donny, like I'm attracted to you because somewhere, deep down, down where it really counts, I have the mind of a mud-wrestler.

CINDY: Don-neee!

DONNY: Now what've I done?

CINDY comes storming out of the bedroom.

CINDY: There is pizza all over the keyboard!

DONNY: (*Wearily.*) Aw-aw. Sorry, Cindy.

CINDY: No way sorry, Donny. Sorry is just not good enough.

DONNY: I'll clean it up.

He heads for the bedroom. She raises a hand.

CINDY: (*Virtually shrieking.*) Don't touch it!

DONNY: You're really pissed aren't you?

CINDY: Just a tad.

DONNY: I'm sooooo bad!

CINDY: Donny, I am fully aware that we live in a consumer oriented society in which built-in obsolescence is a fact of life, where conspicuous waste is the rule, and where everything is instantly disposable... including friends. But that instrument set me back well over a thousand bucks, excluding the interest on the loan, and I intend getting my money's worth before it's chucked in the dumpster.

DONNY: No way, baby. Losing ticket.

CINDY: How come?

DONNY: It's already obsolete. It was obsolete before you carried it through your front door. It was obsolete when you carried it out the shop door. It was obsolete before you even bought it. High-tech moves at an ever increasing speed. Didn't you know that? That's life on spaceship earth as, having safely navigated past the twentieth century, we hurtle blindly on towards the twenty-second. That's if we ever get there, what with climate change, melting glaciers and all those great big holes appearing all over the ozone layer.

DEEDEE: (*Heading towards the arch.*) I'll clean it up. It's my fault anyway. I lost my paper and asked Donny to get it back for me. (*She stops and glances towards the bathroom, moves back to CINDY.*) Your friend's been in there a long time, Cindy. You think he's all right?

CINDY disappears behind the arch.

CINDY: (*Off.*) Josh?... Josh!... Are you okay?... Josh!

JOSH: (*Off, having opened the bathroom door.*) I'm okay.

CINDY: We were getting worried.

She reappears, followed by JOSH looking anything but okay.

DONNY: You don't look okay. Didn't the Ben-gay work?

During the following section JOSH is in one of those predicaments when a person doesn't know whether to laugh or cry, whether to yell or bear one's pain in stoical silence. He finds it difficult to talk and remain composed at the same time.

JOSH: It worked... it worked... my back feels better, much better. Thank you.

CINDY: Then what's wrong? Something's wrong.

JOSH: Wrong?... Ah nothing... nothing... no nothing's wrong.

CINDY: Jo-osh.

JOSH: I'll ah... I'm feeling rather tired. If you'll excuse me I'll call it a day.

CINDY: Not till you tell us what's wrong.

JOSH: I can't.

CINDY: Why not?

JOSH: It's personal. Too personal.

CINDY: Then we're going to sit here and worry ourselves to death. I mean, are you going to die on us?

JOSH: Hardly. No, no, there's nothing for you to worry about.

DEEDEE: You've done something really silly and you're too embarrassed to tell us.

DONNY: (*To DEEDEE.*) Yeh? (*To JOSH.*) Maybe you'd

	like to tell me, man to man.
JOSH:	Oh, what the hell! You're right. I've done a very stupid thing. Well, not really stupid, careless really, thoughtless.
DEEDEE:	Don't cry, please. I can't bear the sight of men crying. I'll never forget the first time I saw my father cry. I truly thought it was the end of the world. I seem to remember I was six at the time.
CINDY:	Deedee…
JOSH:	I'm not crying! I'm in agony!
CINDY:	Why? What did you do?
JOSH:	You're not going to believe this.
DONNY:	Try us.
JOSH:	Well… I rubbed on the Ben-gay… on my back…
DONNY:	Yes?
JOSH:	And then I… I took a pee.
DEEDEE:	So you took a pee. So what?
JOSH:	I wash my hands after taking a pee. This time I should have washed them before, and it's BURNING THE BALLS OFF ME!
CINDY:	(*Trying not to laugh.*) You're kidding.
JOSH:	One does not kid about ultra-sensitive issues.
DEEDEE:	Tissues.

JOSH: What?

DEEDEE: The word you want is "tissues". Ultra-sensitive tissues.

JOSH groans loudly.

Well obviously aspirin isn't going to be much use in this case. Nor Disprin, nor Anacin, Anadin, or Bufferin, Tylanol or Nuprin.

CINDY: Deedee, for Christ's sake! The man is in agony and all you do is stand there quoting from a drugstore catalogue!

DONNY: I had a friend who did that once, only once, in his case it was from chopping chillies. He was cooking Mexican and...

JOSH: What did he do?

DONNY: He ruined the dinner, that's what he did. It isn't easy cooking with one hand.

JOSH: No, what did he do to ease it?

DONNY: Ease what?

JOSH: The condition! The pain. The condition created by the chillies! The condition created by the Ben-Gay!

DEEDEE: The condition created by your own carelessness.

DONNY: (*To DEEDEE.*) Maybe you could find something else to rub on it.

JOSH: Oh, God! I'm dying and I'm surrounded by philosophers, moralists, and comedians.

DONNY: Well, if you must know, he dipped it in a glass of cold water and left it there.

DEEDEE: And went on cooking?

DONNY: With one hand.

DEEDEE: That is disgusting!

DONNY: The means justifies the end. Or is it the other way round? Folk gotta eat.

CINDY: Hold it, everybody!

They all turn and look at her.

I mean just be quiet a minute. (*To DONNY.*) Especially you. If it hadn't been for you none of this would have happened in the first place. (*To JOSH.*) Ice.

JOSH: Definitely not.

DEEDEE: Cucumber is cool.

DONNY: Cucumber is kinky. Hush mah mouf.

CINDY: Cold cream.

DONNY: Butter? Crisco?

JOSH: Bed.

CINDY: What?

JOSH: Is the solution. Forget everything else. If you all will excuse me I'll just retire and let it cool off, in its own good time, as it were.

DONNY: You could walk around outside for a while and give it the cold night air.

CINDY: Don't be ridiculous. There's bound to be a patrol car around and he'll be arrested for indecent exposure.

DONNY: In this cold who would see it? No offence, Josh.

DEEDEE: Are you SURE there's nothing we can do?

DONNY: (*Startled.*) Like what?

JOSH: No no. Nothing. Good-night.

DONNY: Fat chance.

JOSH: What?

DONNY: Of having a good night. Not unless you're into masochism in which case... have a very good night.

JOSH: Yes... well... see you tomorrow. Nice to have met you, Deedee. Yes... well...

He makes an exit with as much grace as he can muster. He has no sooner gone when all three crease up, trying desperately to keep quiet.

DEEDEE: I don't believe it!

CINDY: Shhh! (*To DONNY.*) And you shouldn't be laughing. This is all your fault.

DONNY: I'm sorry. No I really am, Cindy. That's a buddy I've put through the mangle there.

CINDY puts the remaining grocery bags out of sight. DONNY and DEEDEE start giggling again.

CINDY: Okay, that's enough. (*She heads for the second bedroom.*) I'm tired. If you two don't mind I'm calling it a day.

DEEDEE: Cindy, isn't that a bit... well, you know... dangerous?

CINDY: (*Returning with a pile of bedding.*) Dangerous?

DEEDEE stabs a finger in the direction of the first bedroom.

Oh. I'm not sleeping in there. I'm crashing right here. (*She drops the bedding on the floor.*) What're you going to do?

DEEDEE: Oh, my God! My paper!

CINDY: What?

DEEDEE: My USB is still in your computer. Do you think I dare?... No, forget it. Let it bounce about in outer space a while. I'll talk Gardner into giving me an extension.

CINDY: Did you switch off?

DEEDEE: Yeh. You going to see me home, Donny?

DONNY: Sure. (*He heads for the bedroom to collect coats.*)

CINDY: (*Gets cushions from chairs and throws them on the bedding.*) Has Gardner made a pass at you yet?

DEEDEE: No, but he breathes hard.

CINDY: Good sign. You'll get your extension, no sweat.

DEEDEE: Oh, there's plenty of sweat. He does that while he's breathing hard. Usually down my neck. I get goose bumps. I'm only glad he isn't a smoker or into garlic, something like that.

CINDY: Have you and Donny...?

DEEDEE: (*Shakes her head.*) Somehow I can't seem to... I mean, we get so far then... (*She raises both hands and shudders.*)...What about you and Josh?

CINDY shakes her head. DONNY returns wearing his coat and carrying Deedee's. He gives it to her.

DEEDEE: A gentleman would help a lady on with her coat.

DONNY: That's right. (*He heads for the kitchen to pick up his pizza box.*)

DEEDEE: Does that mean he's no gentleman or I'm no lady? (*Seeing the box.*) Where are you taking that?

DONNY: I'm hungry. We can zap it in your microwave.

DEEDEE: (*To CINDY.*) I don't think it's ever going to happen.

CINDY: Ditto.

DONNY: (*At the door.*) You coming?

SCENE THREE - MONDAY MORNING

The front door opens and MARK enters backwards. He is carrying a large cardboard box from the open top of which protrudes a baseball bat. MARK is a solidly built eighteen year old who looks three or four years older. He is wearing overcoat, scarf, gloves, and a woollen ski cap.

He is followed by KRISTEN, also muffled up and carrying another large cardboard box. She seems to chew gum constantly and has a large mouth with which to chew it. It is not always a pretty sight.

MARK: Hey, hey, hey! Anybody home. (*To KRISTEN as he drops his box on the floor.*) Anywhere, anywhere, we'll sort it out later.

KRISTEN puts down her box, starts to take off her coat, etc., which she drops in a chair.

MARK heads back to the hall to re-enter with a window fan and a set of not too new golf clubs which he also deposits on the floor while KRISTEN flicks through a dozen TV channels in quick succession before switching off and wandering into the kitchen to pour two mugs of coffee.

MARK meanwhile goes out into the hall again to return with two large suitcases and a loaded backpack all of which are dumped as KRISTEN takes the two mugs of coffee into the main room puts them down on the table in front of the couch.

KRISTEN: Looks like Cindy's friend's arrived.

MARK: Yep.

KRISTEN: Did you have to bring all this stuff back with you?

MARK: Yep.

KRISTEN: No one will be able to move in here.

MARK: Sure they will. (*He takes a baseball and mitt out of the first box, makes an imaginary pitch, drops them back again.*) And I won't get another chance before the summer.

He takes off his overcoat and ski cap and flops down on the couch, pats the seat beside him, picks up his mug. KRISTEN flops down next to him. They sip their coffee.

KRISTEN: Weird.

MARK: What?

KRISTEN: (*Indicating the bedding.*) That.

MARK: Maybe somebody else crashed here last night. You know what it's like. (*He looks at his watch.*) Pretty good timing, huh?

KRISTEN: Lucky for you you didn't get a ticket.

MARK: My radar works before theirs does.

KRISTEN: Hey, did you read about that woman? She was motoring along when she saw this box at the side of the road and she thought someone had ditched a microwave, so she stopped and put it in the trunk of her car and drove off, and the next thing she knew there were a hundred cops demanding their radar back.

MARK: You are kidding me.

KRISTEN: I read it somewhere. (*She clicks her fingers.*) National Enquirer... I think.

MARK: Now I know you're shitting me. You don't read that stuff.

KRISTEN: Safeway checkout.

MARK: How could the woman be such a dork? It was probably my mother.

KRISTEN: Your mother didn't like me.

MARK: So what? You didn't like her. Who cares? (*He takes off his shoes and socks.*) Maybe she's jealous. (*Sniffs the socks, throws them down, and picks his toes.*)

KRISTEN: You think so?

MARK: (*Shrugs, gets up and crosses to the first box, rummages in it and comes out with a baseball cap which he puts on back to front.*) I don't like her much either. She's too demanding. Too possessive. She's a positive Phaedra as Donny would say. Older people are always so goddam demanding. Do this, do that, don't do this, don't do that. Know what I mean?

KRISTEN: Your dad's nice.

MARK: (*Flopping down beside her again.*) You only say that because he hit on you.

KRISTEN: Oh, shit!

MARK: You know he did.

KRISTEN: I do not!

MARK: I saw. The way he looked at you you were totally naked, baby. From the moment you shook hands to the moment you waved good-bye. I'm not saying I blame him. I wonder when they last got it together. They've slept in separate beds ever since I can remember. Guess it must've all got boring a long time ago. And, man, she's really let herself go! And all the bandannas and bangles, and scarlet nail polish, and lipgloss and hair-do's is never going to hide it. She looks like a Florida freak. Now she's thinking of having injections in her lips. At HER age? Can you imagine her with the Botox look? And, oh God, I wish she wouldn't wear those pink stretch pants. It is truly embarrassing. And the way she rolled her eyes at that waiter last night. Jesus! I wanted to crawl away somewhere and die.

KRISTEN: She was wasting her time anyway.

MARK: How so?

KRISTEN: He was gay.

MARK: How do you know that?

KRISTEN: Oh, come on, Mark! You're not serious.

MARK: I am serious.

KRISTEN: Because you were the one who was totally naked, baby. From the moment you sat down to the moment we walked out the door he was panting to get inside your pants.

MARK: And I didn't even notice. I missed out, huh?

KRISTEN: (*Slapping him playfully.*) Hey! (*And then.*) What a waste though. I thought he was real cute.

MARK: You're not supposed to think anything is cute while I'm around.

KRISTEN: Come off it, macho man, I've seen you strutting your stuff in front off Missy Lucas.

MARK: You cannot be serious!

KRISTEN: Why not? SHE's cute.

MARK: She's sort of okay, if you sort of squint up your eyes, and sort of turn your head away slightly and sort of lower the lights.

KRISTEN: I think your dad's kinda cute too.

MARK: What!

KRISTEN: He is!

MARK: He's bald!

KRISTEN: Isn't that supposed to be a sign of virility?

MARK: Where'd you hear that?

KRISTEN: Read it somewhere.

MARK: National Enquirer?

KRISTEN: Very old Readers Digest, in my dentist's waiting room. With the money he charges you'd think he could afford a few more up to date magazines.

MARK: I'd better tell my mom. I don't think she's noticed how virile he might be... guess she's missing out too, huh? Nah... it wouldn't apply to my dad. He smokes too much.

KRISTEN: What's that got to do with it?

MARK: Smoking really screws up your sex life. Didn't you know that? Causes circulation problems. You can't keep an erection. Every time it stands up the blood drains out and you go limp again. He'd have to dose on Viagra.

KRISTEN: Where'd you hear that?

MARK: Read it somewhere. You're not the only one who stands in checkout lines you know. And he's putting on weight. He's had to let his belt out six notches.

KRISTEN: It suits him. He's tall. He can carry it.

MARK: I don't believe this. He's got bigger hips than my mother. And she's got more cellulite than the moon's got craters.

KRISTEN: Don't exaggerate. Now who's jealous?

MARK: He's the original couch-potato. He's even given up his golf. Look, he gave me his clubs. And,

	talking about potatoes. You hungry?
KRISTEN:	No.
MARK:	Well I am. I'm starving.
KRISTEN:	Ma-ark! We had the most humungous eat as much as you want breakfast not more'n an hour ago.
MARK:	So? I'm hungry. (*He opens a cupboard.*) Hey hey hey!
KRISTEN:	What?
MARK:	This cupboard is full of food.
KRISTEN:	So? It's a food cupboard.
MARK:	This cupboard, ever since I've been in this apartment, has been the sole preserve of Old Mother Hubbard. So how come suddenly it's an amazing cornucopia of canned combustibles?

KRISTEN chokes on her coffee and then shrieks with mirth. MARK stands regarding her till she calms down a little.

	What's so hilarious?
KRISTEN:	You are, Mrs Malaprop.
MARK:	What did I say?
KRISTEN:	The word you want is comestibles. Zip for English. You flunked. Combustible means it burns, it's inflammable.

MARK: Right. Food is made up of calories. You burn calories. Calories are combustibles.

KRISTEN: Bullshit. You don't get out of it that way.

MARK: (*Advancing on her.*) You are so smart, aren't you?

KRISTEN: (*Seeing what is coming, curls her knees up to her chin.*) Pax! Pax! (*Lifts a hand, crosses her fingers.*)

MARK: Zilch on Latin. No pax.

He makes a dive for her. She shrieks and darts off the couch and around the table. He heads her off the other way and catches her over the pile of bedding on the floor, wrestles her to the ground, tickling her, eventually throwing the bedclothes over them both. The movement beneath the clothes gradually subsides. There is a moment and then KRISTEN re-appears. MARK's head follows.

KRISTEN: How come, if he's impotent, he had the hots for me?

MARK: What?

KRISTEN: Your dad. You said...

MARK: Oh, Pavlovian reaction.

KRISTEN: What?

MARK: Pavlov's dogs. Don't you know about Pavlov's dogs? Well, Pavlov was this crazy Frankenstein type Russian scientist and he trained these dogs so that every time they heard a bell ring they thought food was on the way and they would salivate even when there wasn't any... food.

> Eventually papa Pavlov cut off their heads, wired them up with electrodes, and they still salivated even though they didn't have stomachs in which to put the food that wasn't there anyway.

KRISTEN: Yetch! That is gross!

MARK: I know. Poor old dad.

He makes growling noises and throws the covers over them again. After a moment KRISTEN re-appears followed by MARK.

KRISTEN: I hate to tell you this but we've got a class in twenty minutes.

MARK: I know.

He repeats the growling and once more they disappear. Once more the movement beneath the bedclothes subsides. There is a long silence, one or two movements beneath the blankets, then stillness.

JOSH appears from the bedroom. He is wearing only a pair of running shorts and one can see now that he is a man who has actually kept himself in trim; was once an athlete, possibly still is as far as something like tennis or squash goes. He stands for a moment looking around the seemingly empty room, takes in the new assortment of boxes and paraphernalia then, frowning, starts to pick his way towards the kitchen. There is a sudden upheaval beneath the bedclothes and JOSH leaps in twenty directions at once, stubbing a bare toe against something and letting out a yell of agony. The bedclothes are thrown back and the two kids gaze at him as he hops around nursing his toe and finally dropping into a chair.

MARK: Good-morning.

JOSH: What!

MARK: I couldn't think of anything else to say.

JOSH, still nursing his injured toe, draws in his breath through clenched teeth.

            I'm Mark.

KRISTEN: I'm Kristen.

JOSH: I'm in pain.

MARK: (*Getting to his feet.*) I'm really sorry. You think anything's broken?

JOSH: (*Gingerly fingering his toe.*) I don't think so.

MARK: Ice. (*He heads for the fridge.*)

JOSH: What?

MARK: Ice.

JOSH: No! Don't start all that again.

MARK: Huh?

JOSH: I mean, just forget it. (*He notices KRISTEN still gazing at him.*) I'm sorry.

KRISTEN: So am I.

JOSH: No, I mean, I heard you, then I didn't hear you. I thought you'd gone... left... I would have... (*He indicates his naked body, gets to his feet.*) ...

55

	I'll put some clothes on. (*And starts to hobble towards the bedroom.*)
KRISTEN:	No sweat. You look great.
JOSH:	Oh, I'm Josh by the way.
MARK:	We figured. (*There is a silence. Nobody knows what to say.*) I'm Mark and this is Kristen.
JOSH:	You said.
MARK:	Oh… yes. (*Silence.*) Cindy gone to school?
JOSH:	I guess so.

Silence. Then the television starts up downstairs.

	Oh, no!
KRISTEN:	Whatsa matter?
JOSH:	She had that damned thing on till two o'clock this morning and now she's at it again. Will you listen to that?
MARK:	She'll have it like that all day. She's deaf.
JOSH:	She's Jewish.
MARK:	She's lonely.
KRISTEN:	She's old. It keeps her in touch.
JOSH:	Game shows keep her in touch? Reality shows keep her in touch? With what?
KRISTEN:	Excuse me, I've got to go to the bathroom.

JOSH: Will you be long?

KRISTEN stares at him.

I'm sorry, what I mean is... I've just got up, and now that the pain in my foot has subsided somewhat, the pain in my bladder is making itself felt, quite distinctly. We'll soon have an emergency situation here.

KRISTEN: (*With a wave of the hand.*) Go ahead, I can wait.

JOSH: Thank you.

He hobbles out. MARK and KRISTEN look at each other and shrug.

MARK: There is something truly pathetic about a guy with no clothes on, a limp, and a full bladder.

KRISTEN: We'd best get going or we'll be late for class.

MARK: Yeah.

He heads for the couch to put on his shoes and socks. KRISTEN puts on her coat. The phone rings. She answers it.

DEEDEE: Hi! This is Deedee. I know this is probably a stupid question but is Donny there?

KRISTEN: (*Yelling.*) Don-ny! (*Waits.*) No.

DEEDEE: Who's that?

KRISTEN: Doctor Ruth.

DEEDEE: Oh, hi, Kristen! Did you have a great week-end? Tell me all about it.

KRISTEN: You've got to be kidding, Deedee, I don't have time to talk now. We're going to be late for class and you know what a shithead Stanford is for punctuality. If you're not there by the time he's finished calling roll he's just as likely to mark you absent. And the old fucker takes off twenty points every time you blow class. I bet he deducts a hundred points every time his wife says she's got a headache.

MARK: (*Who, by now, should be slipping into his coat.*) Ready?

KRISTEN: Ready. Bye, Deedee. If I see Donny I'll tell him you called.

DEEDEE: Forget it, I'm meeting him in the Union anyway.

KRISTEN: Then what're you calling him for?

DEEDEE: To remind him I'm meeting him in the Union. I'll text him to make sure.

MARK: Come on, come on!

KRISTEN: Gotta go, Deedee.

DEEDEE: Is Josh there?

KRISTEN: Yes, he's in the bathroom.

DEEDEE: AGAIN!

But KRISTEN has put down the phone. MARK, who has collected a couple of books and files from the box

Kristen brought in, opens the door and waits for her.

MARK: Come on, girl! Let's go.

She goes out. He follows, closing the door quietly.

There is a moment and then JOSH reappears from the bathroom. He moves into the room, realises no one is in sight, stops, looks around. He moves further into the room and eyes the pile of bedding with deep suspicion.

JOSH: Mark? (*Silence - except for the TV downstairs*) Kristen? (*He shrugs and goes into the bedroom.*)

Silence. Then the awful sound of a CAT that's just been trodden on, and a yell of pain from JOSH.

Aaaayieee!

An orange thing streaks across the archway.

Jes-us! (*He appears in the archway, following the orange thing.*) Hey, pussy... Here, pussy... Desdemona... I'm sorry, I didn't mean it. Here, stupid cat, where are you? Pss... pss... pss... Kitty kitty kitty... Desdemona... well, fuck you then. (*He reappears in the archway and now we see the red streaks down his shin where the claws got him. He inspects them.*) Phew! Look at that? (*To the Buddha.*) Will you look at that? Will you look at it? I think someone up there's really trying to tell me something. Like get out of here before they carry you out. Antiseptic, antiseptic... when last did I have a tetanus shot... shit! Rabies!

He is heading for the bathroom. The phone rings. He turns back and looks at it.

It's a madhouse!

He goes to the phone. As he puts his hand on the receiver the ringing stops. JOSH takes a deep breath and rolls his eyes heavenwards. Then he moves to the kitchen and starts looking through cupboards. He opens the fridge and looks in there, closes it and stands looking around, obviously perplexed.

The phone rings. He makes a dive for it.

Hello!

CINDY: Josh?

JOSH: Cindy!

CINDY: Just checking to see everything's okay. You were still asleep when I left so I didn't want to disturb you.

JOSH: Thank you.

CINDY: And I thought you might like to meet me for lunch.

JOSH: Fine.

CINDY: I'll come back and pick you up about one.

JOSH: Sure. And, Cindy, talking about food, we bought two loaves of bread last night and I can't find them anywhere.

CINDY: Third drawer from the top.

JOSH: What?

CINDY: Next to the fridge. Gotta fly. Bye!

JOSH: (*Puts down the phone.*) Who in their right mind keeps bread in a drawer? (*Walking over to the unit next to the fridge.*) Especially third from the top. Or one from the bottom. Depending on which way you look at it. (*He pulls open the drawer.*) Five loaves! She already has three loaves and she lets me buy two more! Well at least it widens the choice. (*He takes out a loaf and puts it on the work top, shuts the drawer, opens another one.*) Breadknife... breadknife...

The phone rings.

All right, all right, I give up. Who wants breakfast anyway? (*He goes to the phone, picks it up, barks into it.*) Hello!

DEEDEE: Oh, hi, Josh! It's me, Deedee.

JOSH: (*Voice immediately changing.*) Oh, good morning, Deedee. How are you this morning?

DEEDEE: Just fine. How are you? You're out of the bathroom then.

JOSH looks perplexed.

How's your back?

JOSH: Fine.

DEEDEE: And how's your...

JOSH: FINE!

DEEDEE:	I'm so glad. Listen, is it okay if I come over and retrieve my flash disc from Cindy's computer?
JOSH:	Yeh, sure.
DEEDEE:	Good. I'll be right over.

JOSH stands for a moment looking at the receiver in his hand before putting it down. He is lost in thought a moment longer, then looks down at himself and realises he had better go and put on some clothes. He heads for the bedroom. The DOORBELL rings. He stops in his tracks, turns to face the door.

JOSH:	I don't believe this. I do not believe it. (*The sound of the TV suddenly swells. He looks down at the floor and does a little war dance.*) And will you turn down that fucking noise? Good, Josh, very good. All you need now are shin splints and they really will be carrying you out of here, all the way to the Health Centre for an aspirin. (*The doorbell goes again.*) I'm coming! (*He gets to the door, flings it open, shuts it again quickly, remembering his lack of clothes, opens it again enough to stand behind it and peer around the edge.*) Yes?
DOUGLAS:	(*Voice off.*) Good-morning, sir. My name is Douglas and this is my friend Keith. We're going from door to door, meeting good folk and talking to them about the Bible.
JOSH:	Yes?
DOUGLAS:	May we... er... come in and talk to you?
JOSH:	About God?

DOUGLAS: About His word, yes, and the glory of His kingdom.

JOSH: You're supposed to do that on a Sunday. It's not Sunday.

DOUGLAS: Do you think the devil rests just because it's Monday?

JOSH: Oh, God!

DOUGLAS: Sir?

JOSH: Look, guys, I don't want to seem rude, but I've just got up. I've had one helluva night... I mean, I've had a pretty rough night, I'm not dressed, I'm in no condition right now to discuss God, insurance, or new windows for the patio.

DOUGLAS: Are you feeling all right, sir?

JOSH: No! That's what I'm trying to tell you. Watch my lips.

DOUGLAS: You need the good news, sir, and the peace and happiness that comes with it. God doesn't take note of what day of the week it is, or what people are wearing. We don't mind waiting while you slip into a robe. Our message is too important to stand on ceremony.

JOSH: Why don't you...? Why don't you go see the old lady downstairs? Right below here. She would be delighted to have you visit, I know.

DOUGLAS: We rang the bell, sir, but there's nobody in. The television is on but no one answers the door. Maybe she leaves the TV on to discourage

	burglary. And that's what the devil is, sir, a burglar. He comes like a thief in the night to rob you of your most precious possession, your soul. May we talk about it? May we just come in for a moment? Is a moment too much to ask in exchange for eternal life?
JOSH:	(*Exaggerated sigh.*) Okay. Did you bring the fishies?
DOUGLAS:	I beg your pardon?
JOSH:	I've got the five loaves. Did you bring the fish?
DOUGLAS:	Salvation from sin is no laughing matter, sir. It is not a matter for jokes.
JOSH:	You're right. I'm sorry. That was in very bad taste. It shows you what a state I'm in, right? In no state to talk, that's for sure. So just come back some other time. Next week maybe? (*He starts to close the door.*)
DOUGLAS:	May we leave you some literature then? For a small donation. Not much.
JOSH:	(*Looking further to one side.*) Doesn't Keith ever say anything?
DOUGLAS:	He'll talk if the spirit moves him.
JOSH:	In tongues?
DOUGLAS:	You're joking again, sir.
JOSH:	Well that's the kind of guy I am. Look, fellas, I'll level with you. No point in talking to me anyway because... well... you see... I'm a Buddhist.

DOUGLAS: What?

JOSH: (*Opening the door wider.*) There he is. See Buddha sitting there? See Buddha smile? Buddha talks to me. He's my main man.

He waves a hand in dismissal and starts to close the door again but a well-suited arm appears through the gap, the hand holding a pamphlet.

DOUGLAS: (*Urgently.*) Sir! Please take it. Absolutely no donation is required.

JOSH: Boy, you guys just don't take no for an answer, do you?

DOUGLAS: No one is beyond redemption, sir. If you'll just open your heart, give yourself...

JOSH: Give myself? Okay, now I'll truly level with you. I have to tell you...

DOUGLAS: May I ask your name, sir?

JOSH: What?

DOUGLAS: Your name.

JOSH: Josh.

DOUGLAS: A good Old Testament name.

JOSH: But not a good Old Testament guy.

DOUGLAS: Unburden yourself, Josh, confess your sins. You will feel such release, such joy.

JOSH: THAT is exactly what I am about to do. Since you ask I am going to unburden myself. I have to tell you, Douglas, Keith, that this is a homosexual household... (*He flings wide the door.*) ... and... Hey! Wait! Where' you going? Douglas! Keith! What about my literature? (*He closes the door and chuckles.*) Unburdened. There's more'n one way to skin a cat. (*Moves into the room.*) Josh, you unrepentant sinner, you're doomed, fella, beyond all redemption.

The door flies open again and DEEDEE blows in with a loud "Hi!" From JOSH's reaction there can be no doubt of the start she has given him. He leaps around to face her.

JOSH: Je-SUS! Don't you ever knock?

DEEDEE: Sorry, the door was open.

JOSH: If I spend much longer in this apartment I'm either going to end up with a coronary or I'll be a total basket case.

He sinks down onto the pile of bedding and flops back, knees bent.

DEEDEE: Josh! What have you done to your leg?

She drops her backpack and moves over to him.

JOSH: Hey? Oh, that... cat got me.

DEEDEE sinks to her knees in front of him.

DEEDEE: It looks bad. Did you put something on it?

JOSH: Not yet. I've had a real busy morning.

DEEDEE: Well you'd better get an antiseptic on it fast. Cat's claws are hardly clean you know.

JOSH: Yeh.

DEEDEE: (*Putting a hand on each knee.*) I'll do it for you.

JOSH: Okay, I'll just lie here and die.

But, before DEEDEE can move, the front door opens and DONNY walks in. He stops dead when, from his point of view, he sees an apparently naked JOSH on the floor being intimate with his girl-friend.

BLACKOUT

ACT TWO - TUESDAY.

Deafening Rock music.

MARK, DONNY, and JOSH are around the coffee table playing cards; dealing the cards in the space left on the table between beer cans, ashtrays and cigarette packs. DONNY, who is sitting centre, is considering his hand. The other two wait. Finally Josh gets up and goes over to turn off the music and we see he is sporting a prize-winning black eye. He returns to his seat. Finally MARK looks up from his own hand, pushes his baseball cap to the back of his head and glares at DONNY, scratches his head, and then prods DONNY's shin with his bare toes.

MARK: Come on, Smeg, what're you waiting for? Wake up and smell the coffee, man.

DONNY: I can't decide, man.

MARK looks at JOSH, expressing impatience. DONNY finally makes a decision, pulls two cards, lays them down, keeps three in his hand.

Two.

JOSH deals him the cards. DONNY's face lights up like a Christmas tree. The other two exchange looks while DONNY tries to recover and appear casual.

Ah... yeah... ah. (*Suddenly noticing.*) Hey! I got no more chips, man!

MARK: So?

DONNY: So can I borrow some?

MARK: You owe me ten bucks already. You want some more chips, buy 'em. No checks.

DONNY: How am I supposed to bet if I got nothing to bet with?

MARK: You wanna bet?

JOSH: How much do you want to bet, Donny?

DONNY: You gonna stake me?

JOSH: Depends. How much you want to bet?

DONNY: (*Thinking hard, in old Western B. movie style saloon*) We-ell now... I was reckoning on opening ... for... I dunno... say... (*To Mark.*) How much do I owe you?

MARK: You know how much you owe me, sphincter muscle. Get on with it.

DONNY: Okay I'll open for five bucks.

MARK throws in his hand. JOSH does likewise. DONNY stares at them in disbelieving amazement.

DONNY: (*Squeaking.*) What're you doing? What're you guys doing?

MARK: What does it look like, dickhead?

DONNY: You mean you're not playing?

MARK: Not this hand we're not.

DONNY: You can't do that!

He looks from MARK to JOSH who shakes his head.

MARK: If you wanna be where the men are, Donny, who go out and drink beer and puke and fart and belch, you gotta learn to control your knee-jerk reactions.

DONNY: What're you talking about?

JOSH: What Mark is trying to say....

MARK: Hey! Since when did I need an interpreter? I know what I'm trying to say.

JOSH: ... he's telling you that, if you're going to play poker, you've got to have a poker face. Shouldn't be too difficult for you. You're an actor after all. What'd you have anyway?

DONNY: You're not going to believe this.

MARK: Oh yes we are. Why the hell you think we threw in our hands?

DONNY: Four fucking aces! That's amazing, man! What are the odds? A zillion to one. For the first and probably the only time in my fucking life I've got four fucking aces and you chickens chicken out. It'll never happen again. Never! Excuse me while I go outside and kill myself.

MARK: I knew a guy once killed himself playing cards. Broke his neck.

JOSH: Sounds highly improbable.

MARK: I'm not kidding.

DONNY: Playing cards?

MARK: Sure.

DONNY: You're shitting us, man.

MARK: I swear to God! He was playing bridge, and was going for a slam, and when he saw he'd got the last trick, he got so excited he threw down his card like that... (*He demonstrates, whipping a card onto the table.*) ... and broke his neck. (*His head flops to one side.*)

DONNY: So how come you haven't just broken your neck? Anyway nobody gets that excited playing bridge.

MARK: You've obviously never played bridge with bridge players.

DONNY: I knew a guy got killed by a passing vehicle never even touched him.

MARK: How was that?

DONNY: I saw it happen, man. This ninety year old dude was just about to step off the kerb when this ambulance comes flying by and the driver sounds off his siren, Wee-ya, wee-ya, wee-ya! And this guy drops dead of a heart attack on the spot. And you know what made it worse?

MARK: How could it be worse if the guy was dead?

DONNY: Ironic, man, ironic. It was an Advanced Life-Support System Vehicle. A million dollars worth of high-tech life-saving equipment goes disappearing down the street and there's this poor old John Doe lying dead in the gutter.

MARK: You should have given him the kiss of life.

DONNY: I don't give live guys kisses. I'm not about to start kissing dead ones. Anyway, there were a lot of other people around.

JOSH: There always are.

They wait for him to elaborate. He doesn't.

MARK: I knew a guy back home killed himself smoking.

DONNY: People die from smoking all the time.

MARK: I didn't say he DIED from smoking, asshole, I said he KILLED himself smoking. Seems like his wife wouldn't let him smoke in the house so he climbed out of a window onto the porch roof. Porch gave way, down he went, broken neck.

DONNY: Was it the same guy broke his neck playing cards?

MARK: You don't believe a thing I say, do you?

DONNY: Because you're full of shit.

MARK: We got any more beer?

He gets up and goes to the fridge.

DONNY: Life's a bitch and no mistake.

MARK: We're not talking life here, Donny, we're talking death and that is heavy, man.

DONNY: (*Points his index finger at JOSH's head.*) Bang! Hey, I'm real sorry about the eye, Josh.

JOSH: I thought they only came in threes.

DONNY: What?

JOSH: Accidents, disasters, catastrophes. Guess I was mistaken. (*Pointing to his eye.*) This makes four.

MARK: (*Returning to the table with a bottle and three glasses.*) No more beer.

DONNY: That makes five.

MARK: But there's some Mad Dog left. You ever had Mad Dog, Josh?

JOSH: Not that I can recall.

MARK: It's awesome. You'll really dig this stuff, man.

DONNY: So long as you don't get totally trashed on it. I tell you, man, you get smashed on this shit it'll make you laser puke like you could hit a nickel at ten feet.

MARK pours them each a glass.

JOSH: Sounds Dionysian.

DONNY: Sounds more like substance abuse to me.

MARK: You could do with some soap abuse that's what you could do with. Why don't you go jack off a nice big bar of soap?

DONNY: Why don't we send out for a nice big pizza?

MARK: Your treat?

DONNY: Are you kidding? I got no money. You guys have taken me to the cleaners.

MARK: Somebody ought to do that. I can take you in small doses, Donny. Trouble is you always come in large ones. Go take a shower. Shampoo your pits.

DONNY: Get off my case, shithead. Whose deal?

MARK: What do you mean, whose deal? You got no money how do you expect to play cards?

MARK and JOSH raise their glasses. DONNY moves away.

Where you going?

DONNY: You kill me, man. If we're not playing cards and we're not eating I'm going to learn some words. Real life must go on. (*He leaves.*)

MARK: That pig's a basket case.

JOSH: I'm beginning to think we're all basket cases.

MARK: Hurts real bad, huh?

JOSH: (*Touching his eye.*) No, funnily enough, doesn't hurt at all.

MARK: That's not what I'm talking about.

JOSH: Oh. (*Pause.*) We're talking life again, are we? Any life in particular? Or just life in general?

MARK: Whatever. It's shit.

JOSH: You speak from your own vast experience of course.

MARK: I speak from my eyes and ears.

JOSH: Sounds like a unique malformation.

MARK: Come on, Josh! You know what I mean. I see and hear all the crap that goes on around me. What I learn in class goes towards my degree. What I learn out of class goes towards my education. Take you for instance...

JOSH: I'd rather you didn't.

MARK: I've learned a lot since you got here. You want to hear about it?

JOSH: No thank you.

MARK: Why not? You might learn something too.

JOSH: About myself?

MARK: Sure. Why not? You think an eighteen year old's got nothing to teach you?

JOSH: On the contrary, there are plenty of eighteen year olds who have plenty to teach me. But the only thing this particular eighteen year old can tell me about me is that I'm a prick and no prick wants to be told he's a prick. That's what you're aiming...

MARK: Okay, forget I spoke. No offence and enjoy your

stay. Just because you're a prick doesn't mean to say I don't like you.

JOSH: Thank you.

MARK: You're welcome. You didn't like me though, did you? When you first met me?

JOSH: No.

MARK: It's the image. Everyone takes me for a total jock. I keep the poetry in my soul to myself. You thought I was a jock didn't you?

JOSH: No.

MARK: You didn't?

JOSH: I thought you were a jerk.

MARK: Yes, well there you are then. You're a prick and I'm a jerk. Mutual understanding is a great thing.

JOSH: Yes. I'd really like to understand Cindy more than I do.

MARK: What you mean is, you'd like to understand Cindy more in relation to yourself. Or, to put it more succinctly, how's the best way to hit on her.

JOSH: You think that's all it is?

MARK: What else?

JOSH: What if I were to say I'm in love with her?

MARK: I'd say you're an even bigger prick than you think you are.

JOSH: Why's that?

MARK: How's your wife?

JOSH: What?

MARK: Does she know where you are, who you're with, and what you're up to?

JOSH stares at him.

She knows where you are but not who you're with or what you're up to. What did you tell her? You're on a seminar or something? Cindy ever mention your wife?

JOSH: No. (*He takes a large gulp of his MD.*)

MARK: Never? Now why is that do you suppose? She's mentioned your wife to me. That's how I know you got one. Would you leave your wife for Cindy?

JOSH: I've thought about it.

MARK: You've thought about it.

JOSH: Now look...

MARK: No way, man. The lay's the thing, as the Danish dude once said. That's all there is. If it weren't Cindy it would be any of a dozen other attractive chicks.

JOSH drains his glass, goes to pour himself another.

You know it, even if you don't want to admit it. Cindy knows it, and she doesn't want it. And, even if it WERE more than that, Josh, it'd never work.

JOSH: (*Icily.*) Really. Tell me more.

MARK: (*Finger to his lips.*) Some other time.

The front door opens and CINDY and DEEDEE enter. There is a general round of "Hi!" and "How ya doin'?" as the girls drop their backpacks and CINDY flops into the nearest available chair.

CINDY: Shit! What a day.

JOSH takes a drink.

MARK: You guys seen Kristen?

DEEDEE: Yeh, she's over at the library.

MARK: Great. I'll go join her. Then we'll go eat.

He goes to the bedroom to get his things to go out.

Hey, Donny, Deedee's here.

DEEDEE: So what kind of a day did you have, Josh?

JOSH: For the most part (*looking at CINDY*) solitary.

CINDY gives him a wry look as she gets up and goes to the kitchen to get herself a soda.

DEEDEE: I'm real sorry about the eye, Josh. How does it feel now?

JOSH: It's all right.

DEEDEE: You know I didn't mean it. I was aiming at Donny and you just sorta got in the way.

JOSH: No, Deedee, I didn't get in the way. I'm just not as speedy as Donny in taking evasive action, that's all. And that's quite a pitching arm you got there. They ought to recruit you for the Cubs.

CINDY: You don't have to keep on about it, Deedee. He's not going to sue. (*Uncertain.*) Are you?

DEEDEE: I'm just making sure he's got the facts of the case.

CINDY: The facts of the case are that, if you folk'll excuse me, I'm going to take a shower. Is it safe to leave you alone?

DEEDEE: So long as you lock Donny in his room on the way to the bathroom.

CINDY: I've got a better idea. You've had a go with the ball, now take a turn with the bat. You might connect with the right person this time. Guess this is turning into your personal Brave New World, huh, Josh? What can I say?

She goes. JOSH takes another slug of MD.

JOSH: So.

DEEDEE: So.

JOSH: And how was the rest of your day after The Little Big Horn?

DEEDEE: Huh?

JOSH: Oh, come on, every American child knows where Custer made his last stand. And I'm beginning to know exactly how he felt.

DEEDEE: (*Touching her eye.*) You mean...

JOSH: Among other things. I could have gone to Mexico. Montezuma's revenge would have been a piece of cake compared to this. So how WAS your day?

DEEDEE: Terrible. I had to let that grease ball, Gardner, breathe ALL over me to get my extension. I mean he was that close! (*She holds up a hand, thumb and forefinger about half an inch apart.*) And Donny has been a total pain in the butt. The fascination with sleaze is disappearing fast. I think I'm going to blow him off and go for some clean-cut macho scholarship football player from the business school instead. A jock who wears Brooks Brothers shirts. It might not be so intellectually stimulating but there's an alternative fascination in beautiful hulk wouldn't you say?

JOSH: Not being into hulk I really wouldn't know.

DEEDEE: Though I believe I could, before leaving college, have an affair with a member of faculty. Only we don't have any attractive ones here, not even in the younger set. They're all nerds. And it's the older ones who are as horny as hell. Like Gardner. He's lived with the same woman for thirty-five years...

JOSH winces visibly.

... and he's totally bored with her.

JOSH: You don't know that. He might love her very much.

DEEDEE: Nevertheless he's totally bored with her and he's looking for extra-curricular activity. Maybe I'll wait till I go to grad school. You ever have an affair with one of your students, Josh?

JOSH: No. (*He drains his glass and pours another.*)

DEEDEE: I bet you've been tempted though, huh?

JOSH: (*Amused.*) Maybe.

DEEDEE: What kind of girls turn you on?

JOSH: Sexy ones.

DEEDEE: Well of course, that goes without saying. To go for non-sexy ones would be perversion. But what do you find sexy? Describe a girl in one of your classes you've got the hots for. I mean, do you like beanpoles? Or slap the fat and ride the ripples?

JOSH nearly chokes on his drink.

Come on, tell me. Do your students all love you? I bet they do.

JOSH: You wouldn't be flirting with me, young lady, would you?

DEEDEE: Mois? Under my best friend's roof? And with

my about-to-be-ex-boyfriend sulking in the next room? Though I have to admit... (*She trails off.*)

JOSH: Don't even think about it. (*Pause.*) Though I have to admit... (*He trails off.*)

MARK returns, ready to go.

DEEDEE: Mark, what IS Donny doing?

MARK: Learning lines.

DEEDEE: Good. (*She picks up her backpack.*) You wanna walk me home on the way to the library?

MARK: (*A moment of surprise, then.*) Sure. See you later, Josh.

JOSH nods.

DEEDEE: See you later.

They go out. JOSH stands for a moment, looks around the empty room.

JOSH: (*To the Buddha*). Well, looks like it's just you and me again, old buddy. What are we going to talk about this time? Seems to me like we're fast running out of conversation here. (*He pours another glass of MD.*) Men younger than me head multi-nationals, they're billionaire televangelists, or they become president of the United States even. What are my genes doing to me for Christ sake? This is ridiculous. Oh, pardon me... (*He holds out his glass.*) ...Would you care for one? No, of course not. Silly question. Alcohol is strictly for the unenlightened, huh?

An anodyne for blue balls.

DONNY: (*Appearing in the arch.*) For what?

JOSH waves a hand and moves away.

Where's Deedee?

JOSH: Gone.

DONNY: Oh? Gone long?

JOSH: I really didn't take any notice of the time, Donny, but I would estimate about a minute. Learnt all your lines?

DONNY: Sort of.

JOSH: Your heart isn't really in it, is it?

DONNY: Yeh, well I guess that's something I'm gonna have to get used to. If you're going to make your bread in the theatre you can't play Hamlet all the time. I just don't dig this Absurdist shit.

JOSH: I'm beginning to. It seems less and less absurd and makes more and more sense with every passing minute.

DONNY: You reckon.

JOSH: I reckon.

DONNY: This theatre where you met Cindy, where you're a director...

JOSH: Uh-uh-uh-uh-uh. I'm not a director, Donny. It's a community theatre, and I'm on the board,

	which means I go to meetings and think of ways of getting money out of people to keep the place going, tax deductible.
DONNY:	Yes but, if you're on the board, you got influence. You think you can get me a job there when I graduate?
JOSH:	You could audition like everybody else.
DONNY:	But you could put in a word for me. Hey! I got a great idea.
JOSH:	We'll put on a show! We could turn the barn into a theatre and I got a couple of old paintings I could sell! (*Seeing DONNY's puzzled face.*) Before your time, Donny, movies before your time.
DONNY:	I seen plenty old movies.
JOSH:	Micky Rooney? Judy Garland?
DONNY:	Shit, no! I don't dig musicals. No, what I was going to say was, why don't you come to rehearsal tomorrow?
JOSH:	Okay. (*Then, more enthusiastically.*) Sure, why not? Give me something to do other than read, watch reruns, walk around this dreary town in temperatures that would freeze the balls off old Buddha here.
DONNY:	I don't think he's got any, poor bastard.
JOSH:	Lucky bastard.
DONNY:	What?

JOSH: Nothing.

DONNY: It's okay, you're not the only one who's got them. Three quarters of the student body are in the same state. Last night three of us cruised round for about four hours. We sat in the car and talked girls girls girls, sex sex sex. It got so steamed up in there it was like the Turkish bath scene in Orson Welles' Othello. I'm telling you, man, my relationship with Deedee is so non-sexual it's become positively sexual. Does that make sense?

JOSH: Perfect sense.

DONNY: You old guys don't know how lucky you are, man. You got your rocks off when you didn't have to fear for your life every time you had a fuck.

JOSH: You've had a lot of fearful moments then.

DONNY: Well... no... but the way things are going I'm not likely to, am I?

JOSH: How many times have you had that fearful moment, Donny?

DONNY: (*After a pause and somewhat abashed.*) Once.

JOSH: Like your four aces.

DONNY: Don't say that!

JOSH: What happened?

No response beyond a deep frown.

No, I'm interested.

DONNY: Well, we were partying. It was a pick-up. I was drunk. She was drunk. I don't remember too much about it to tell the truth. It was a one night stand. But it worried the shit out of me afterwards. This was when I was a sophomore so that tells you something. Then I couldn't stand it any longer. I mean, I'd heard so many stories, like people finding out they'd got it and deliberately screwing around, that kinda thing. So I got myself tested. I mean it's still out there isn't it? I mean you never can tell as George Bernard Shaw said.

JOSH: It came back negative of course, the test.

DONNY: Yep. Negative. You know how I felt? Like I could fly, man. But now, every time it gets to the point... I mean, I know this isn't New York or L.A. or Frisco, or Washington DC but this thing spreads, man, and kids at this university come from those places, and something inside of me says, "Whoa, back off there, man." And where's the romance when you want to hit on someone and have to start asking questions like who have they slept with and when and how often? And did they know the people they slept with and the people who slept with the people they slept with. I mean, man, when even big sports dudes can get it, you know? What kind of a deal are we kids getting here? And you know what I think is the shittiest bit? The things that are causing this havoc aren't even alive, man! Nucleic acid and protein. It doesn't make any sense.

JOSH: Totally absurd, huh? (*Pointing to the Buddha.*)

                    Now you know why he's so lucky not to have any.

CINDY appears in the arch. She is wrapped in a bright kimono and her hair is swathed in a towel.

CINDY: Who's lucky not to have any what?

DONNY: Oh, hi, Cindy! How ya doin'?

CINDY: (*Advancing into the room.*) You didn't answer my question.

JOSH: Enjoy your shower? You weren't in very long.

CINDY: I just needed to freshen up. You know what I could go for?

DONNY: Food. How about Chinese? We haven't eaten Chinese in a long time.

CINDY: Nope. This is what I need now.

She has taken down a cookie jar from the top of the fridge, sits down and takes out a bong, looks in the bowl, it is obviously still smokable. She lights it with a cigarette lighter, takes a deep drag and passes the pipe to DONNY who hasn't taken his eyes off it. He takes a drag and, after a moment, passes the pipe to JOSH who shakes his head. They both look at him.

DONNY: You don't?

JOSH: No.

DONNY: Never?

JOSH: Oh, I tried it a couple of times, but it never

	seemed to do anything for me, so... (*He shrugs.*)
DONNY:	This is good shit, man. This'll do something for you. Go ahead, try it.
JOSH:	Well... okay... why the hell not? But it won't do anything for me so really it's a waste. (*He takes the pipe, takes a drag, holds it in, passes the pipe to DONNY.*)
DONNY:	Is that the best or isn't it?
CINDY:	Aaah... THAT is GOOD. I begin to feel like a human being again
JOSH:	(*Letting go and taking a deep breath.*) Instead of what?
CINDY:	Total garbage.

DONNY passes the pipe back to JOSH who accepts it and takes another drag before passing it on to CINDY who does likewise.

JOSH:	(*After a long moment during which he seems to be paralysed.*) Oh, God!

They turn to look at him.

DONNY:	Whatsa matter?
JOSH:	I feel sick. I'm going to be sick.

He gets to his feet and weaves his unsteady way towards the bathroom. They watch him go.

DONNY:	Well dip me in shit! I didn't expect it to do that for him.

There is the sound of violent retching from the bathroom.

> Maybe he's got an allergy or something. (*Suddenly noticing the MD bottle, he picks it up and looks at it.*) Oh, no, he doesn't. Will you look at that? I warned him and he's almost killed the whole thing! The man's got no self-control.

More retching is heard, if anything even more violent than before.

> Guess this... (*The pipe.*) ... on top of the Mad Dog was the last straw... pardon me ... grass... that broke the camel's back.

He takes another pull, passes the pipe to CINDY. They smoke contentedly while, in the bathroom, JOSH pukes his guts out.

SCENE FIVE - WEDNESDAY MORNING

The phone is ringing. It could FADE UP as though gradually impinging on someone's consciousness and it needs to ring a good while to give the actor JOSH enough time for his change. Eventually he appears from the bedroom, wearing his running shorts, inadequately wrapped in Cindy's kimono, and looking like death. He staggers to the phone and croaks into it.

JOSH: Yes?

CINDY: Josh? Where've you been? I've been calling for hours. I tried your phone but couldn't get through.

JOSH: I was in bed. I think I had the pillow over my head. (*He groans and puts a hand to it.*) Oooh... it hurts. Anyway, I forgot to charge the phone last night which is why you didn't get anywhere. Such is modern technology. It's dead as a doornail and I wish I were.

CINDY: Are you awake?

JOSH: Sort of, I suppose, and I wish I weren't.

CINDY: There's seltzer in the bathroom cabinet. Now listen up good. This is an emergency. Dr Gardner's on his way over.

JOSH: On his way over where?

CINDY: To the apartment for Christ's sake! Where else? Now listen...

JOSH: What's he coming here for? (*He tries to look at his watch.*) At this... Good God! Is that the...?

CINDY: Josh! This is no time for talk. He's coming over to look at the computer. There's a gremlin in it and I can't sort it out. God! I hope it's not a virus. It's probably Pizzaritis. So do me a favour will you? You know the plants in the bedroom...

JOSH: Plants?

CINDY: On the windowsill... the plants on the windowsill!

JOSH: The beautiful pale green ones that got away from your black thumb.

CINDY: God, how innocent can you get? Josh, please! This is as serious as a stroke. Hide them somewhere.

JOSH: Hide them?

CINDY: (*Almost screaming.*) Hide them!

JOSH: There's no need to get hysterical, Cindy.

CINDY: I am not getting hysterical there is every reason to get hysterical! HIDE THEM!

JOSH: Hide them where?

CINDY: Anywhere! So long as they're out of sight when Gardner gets there.

JOSH: Gotcha.

CINDY: I'll be over as soon as I can.

JOSH: How long before...? (*But she has hung up.*) Cindy? Cindy!

But the line is dead. He is still holding the receiver and looking slightly bewildered when the DOORBELL rings. He looks towards the door, looks at the phone in his hand, looks around the room, looks down at himself, puts down the phone and starts for the bedroom. The DOORBELL goes again followed by imperious knocking. Dr Gardner is someone obviously not used to being kept waiting. JOSH stops in mid-flight, wraps the kimono around him as far as it will go and, making for the door, flings it open. His tone is breezily welcoming to the point of embarrassment.

Good-morning, good-morning! You must be

	Dr Gardner. Come in, come in. I was expecting you.

JOSH stands aside, holding open the door, and GARDNER enters. He is short, chubby - to put it kindly - bearded, and with heavy horn-rimmed glasses. He is immaculately dressed in dark suit, collar and tie beneath his winter coat, scarf, and gloves.

GARDNER:	(*Hardly believing what he sees.*) And you are Dr Armstrong.
JOSH:	That's right.

He holds out his hand but GARDNER is busy taking off his gloves and ignores it.

	Only it isn't right. I mean, it isn't DOCTOR Armstrong. No. I never took a terminal degree. I might be terminal in other directions but not degree wise. Ha ha ha. No, it's professor I'm afraid, associate professor in fact. I'm sorry about the ah... (*He indicates the kimono.*)... When I said I was expecting you, what I should have said was, Cindy's just this minute called to say that I SHOULD expect you and I didn't have a chance to... put any clothes on.
GARDNER:	Well perhaps you'd care to do so now. And, while you're doing it, I can take a look at the computer. (*He looks at his watch.*) I don't have that much time so if you'd be so kind as to show me where it is?

He takes a step towards the arch but JOSH quickly bars his way and then moves sideways towards the kitchen, keeping a wary eye on his visitor.

JOSH: Ah... wouldn't you?... Would you care for a cup of coffee? Ah, tea? Something stronger?

GARDNER: No thank you. I'm not much of a drinking man, Professor Armstrong.

JOSH: Call me Josh, please.

GARDNER: Particularly in the middle of the day. I do my best to dissuade both faculty colleagues and members of the student body from drinking as well. Alcohol abuse is something I cannot tolerate. (*He looks meaningfully at the MD bottle.*) I take it you might not agree with my sentiments but this is a religiously endowed university and we have the highest moral standards to maintain. Not easy in a department of drama. It seems to me that substance abuse and deviation are the twin curses of the modern world. Are you married, Professor Armstrong?

JOSH: Yes I am. How about you?

GARDNER: Children?

JOSH: No children. How about you?

GARDNER: Oh yes. I have a son of eleven, Langley by name. That was the name of his maternal grandfather. (*He fishes in his breast pocket for a wallet from which he produces a photograph which he passes over.*) This was not merely in deference to my lovely wife but because the judge was a wonderful wonderful man. A pillar of rectitude and a solid member of his church and community.

From JOSH'S reaction to the photograph he is not too impressed with the young Langley. He hands it back.

	And two little girls, all extremely bright I'm happy to say and perfectly normal.
JOSH:	Ten toes, ten fingers. Each I mean, not between them.
GARDNER:	(*Replaces the photograph and takes another step towards the arch.*) Now, if you don't mind...
JOSH:	Judge Langley... I know that name.
GARDNER:	Arkansas.
JOSH:	Yes, I seem to remember... wasn't there something odd... peculiar about his death?
GARDNER:	Peculiar?
JOSH:	Didn't I read something in the papers?
GARDNER:	Oh, come now, Professor Armstrong, you don't believe everything you read in the papers do you?
JOSH:	And there was a lot of rumour...
GARDNER:	Innuendo! Defamation! What great ones do the less will prattle of and not without malice.
JOSH:	He was known for his racist sentiments I believe.
GARDNER:	No, no, he was NOT a racist! Most certainly not. He was a good old-fashioned Southern Baptist who believed in the Bible and...

The door flies open and CINDY enters breathlessly.

CINDY: I'm sorry I'm sorry. Would you believe the car broke down? Wro-ong! It wouldn't even start. Battery flat. Like your phone. Finally got one of the maintenance staff to give me a jump start. Anyway, here I am. What are you doing in my kimono?

JOSH: Looking ridiculous. I didn't bring a robe and this was all I could find.

This is the first time GARDNER has taken his eyes off CINDY and she uses it as an opportunity to make signals to JOSH - has he hidden the plants? He can't respond because GARDNER is now watching him.

CINDY: Well, hadn't you better get dressed?

GARDNER turns to look at her. JOSH shakes his head - No, he hasn't hidden the plants.

JOSH: Yes, I suppose so.

GARDNER turns to look at him. CINDY makes signs for him to go and hide them, double quick.

CINDY: Well go on then. Doctor Gardner wants to get in there to the computer.

JOSH: Yes, well, if you'll excuse me...

He backs away, turns, and disappears into the bedroom. GARDNER looks at his watch.

GARDNER: I hope he isn't going to be too long, Cindy. I really don't have that much time.

CINDY: I don't think he looks ridiculous. I think he looks rather sweet in my kimono.

GARDNER: Sweet?

CINDY: Pathetic. Like a sick puppy.

GARDNER: Cindy, I did not come here to discuss what Professor Armstrong looks like in a kimono. Personally I find it neither sweet or pathetic. In fact I find it rather revolting if you must know. You don't agree of course.

CINDY: What?

During GARDNER's speech JOSH has appeared in the arch carrying a potted plant and heading for the bathroom. CINDY shakes her head violently. JOSH shakes his head in turn, questioning, shrugs and goes back to the bedroom.

GARDNER: Is something wrong?

CINDY: Wrong?

GARDNER: You're shaking.

There is a clatter from the bedroom. GARDNER looks towards the arch.

GARDNER: Your friend is a noisy dresser.

There is more clatter.

(*Losing control.*) What the hell is he doing? I beg your pardon.

CINDY lets out a cry. GARDNER startled, turns back to her.

CINDY: I feel... sort of... (*She puts her hand to her forehead and sways a little.*) ...dizzy. You know? Must have been standing around in the cold trying to get the car going. I'll be okay in a minute.

GARDNER: (*Solicitously taking her arm and guiding her to a chair.*) Here, you'd best sit down.

CINDY: Yes. I'm sorry about all this.

GARDNER: Shhhh... it's all right, my dear, it's quite all right.

CINDY: (*Loudly.*) I'm sure Josh won't be long!

GARDNER: I hope not. I've got a lot to get through today and a faculty meeting this afternoon. Maybe I'd best just get in there and get on with it.

He heads for the bedroom. CINDY lets out another little squeal. He turns back.

What is it?

CINDY: Faint... faint... (*She sways in the chair.*)

GARDNER: (*Returns to her, takes her hand and rubs it.*) Is there anything I can do?

CINDY: Maybe... ah... maybe... a... a hot drink would help. Do you think? Yes. I'll make myself...

She starts to get up. He restrains her.

GARDNER: No, you stay right there. I'll do it. What do you want?

CINDY: Well there's some herb tea in the cupboard.

GARDNER: Herb tea.

CINDY: Top shelf, next to the fridge, pretty box with flowers on it.

GARDNER heads for the kitchen, shaking his head in disbelief. JOSH appears in the arch, smiling broadly.

JOSH: Okay, you can go in now.

GARDNER: (*Staring at him.*) You're not dressed!

JOSH: What? Oh... no... I gathered up my things and I can dress in the bathroom.

GARDNER: Couldn't you have done that in the first place?

JOSH: I didn't think of it in the first place.

GARDNER: Well?

JOSH: Well what?

GARDNER: Your things! Your things!

JOSH: Oh, yes, my things. Good thinking, Batman.

He disappears into the bedroom. GARDNER turns to look at CINDY, his expression questioning, "This is a professor?"

JOSH reappears with his shoes and a bundle of clothes.

GARDNER marches briskly into the bedroom followed by CINDY. JOSH gives her a beaming smile and a little wave of the fingers as she passes but her response is to growl and claw the air with her hands.

JOSH shrugs, moves into the room and drops his stuff on a chair. Then he moves on into the kitchen.

Coffee, coffee, I need coffee.

The front door opens and DONNY enters, throws down his backpack.

DONNY: Shit!

JOSH: Shit?

DONNY: That's what I said.

JOSH: Yes, I know it's what you said, but what does it mean? Is it not, I think you will agree, the most overworked word in America?

DONNY: Maybe that's because it covers everything.

JOSH: Literally? Or figuratively? Want a caffeine fix? Make you feel better.

DONNY: I got bad news for you.

JOSH: I don't think I can take it.

DONNY: All the coffee in this place is unleaded.

JOSH: I'll drink it all the same. Could have a psychological effect.

DONNY: So thanks for making rehearsal, friend!

JOSH: What? Oh, shit!

DONNY: Yeh. Right on.

JOSH: I'm sorry, Donny. Guess I just wasn't up to it.

DONNY: By the look of you you're not up to anything. You look like shit.

JOSH: You know something? We could have an entire conversation using nothing but that word. The intonation, inflexion, that would give your exact meaning without the need for anything more. I take it, for example, by your first utterance that (a) you feel like death, (b) the rehearsal was a mess, and (c) you think I'm a real bastard for not having been there. Three meanings in one little four letter word. Now that, as you might say, is totally awesome.

DONNY: You're talking shit.

JOSH: I guess so.

DONNY: Deedee hasn't been around has she?

JOSH: I haven't seen her.

DONNY picks up the phone, lets it drop. JOSH holds out the mug of coffee he has poured.

Things not going so good?

DONNY: (*Taking the coffee.*) You could say that.

JOSH: On the other hand you could simply say...

BOTH: SHEE-IT!

CINDY darts into the arch, glares at them, and darts off again.

DONNY: What's eating her?

JOSH: I would say Doctor Gardner's eating her. Or rather I think maybe he'd like to.

DONNY: Doctor...!

JOSH: (*Finger to lips.*) Shhh. (Whispering.) He's - in - there.

DONNY: No shit!

JOSH: I shit you not.

DONNY: What the fuck's he doing here?

JOSH: My, my, a different four letter word. Our vocabulary stretches to new horizons.

DONNY: What's he doing?

JOSH: It would appear, Donny, that, when it comes to computers, our good doctor really knows his shit.

DONNY: What are you doing in Cindy's kimono?

JOSH: That's the second time I've been asked that.

DONNY: Did he see you like that? Holy shit!

JOSH: An adjective yet. You know, as a professor of history, maybe I should write the definitive history of scatology. I could go down in history myself as the Kinsey of crap; the butt, no pun intended, of every bad asshole joke in the world.

DONNY: Jesus! You feel worse than I do.

JOSH: And that's no shit. So tell me about your lousy rehearsal. It might make me feel better.

DONNY: Why don't you put some clothes on? That might make you look better.

JOSH: True, true, I'll do that.

JOSH picks up his clothes and is about to head for the bathroom when there is a clatter and a yell from the bedroom. He runs to the arch and looks off. There is a long silence and then GARDNER storms out of the bedroom. His face, shirt front, and suit are spotted with wet earth. Obviously the plants have recently been well watered. He storms by JOSH, picks up his coat, scarf, and gloves, and storms out.

A distraught CINDY appears in the arch. For a moment it is a tableau and then...

ALL 3: SHIT!

SCENE SIX - THURSDAY AFTERNOON.

DONNY is eating pizza at the kitchen table.

MARK and KRISTEN, barefooted, are either end of the couch and playing tootsie. They each have a book. DONNY regards them for a moment.

DONNY: Wouldn't you two have more fun sucking face?

MARK: You can't suck face and read at the same time.

He tickles KRISTEN's sole with his toes. She giggles and hastily withdraws the foot.

You can feed face and read at the same time and, like I always say, to each his own so find yourself a good book and leave us alone.

KRISTEN: How's the play going, Donny?

DONNY: Don't ask.

KRISTEN: Okay, I won't.

DONNY: The man calls himself a director. He couldn't direct traffic in a one horse town. You know why he speaks the way he does? Everybody thinks it's because he's got adenoids. Well I've got news for you. Those adenoids are haemorrhoids because the man talks through his asshole.

MARK: Listen to this. This is the voice of perscipacity speaking.

KRISTEN: (*Shrieking.*) The voice of what?

MARK: You heard me.

KRISTEN: I heard you. And I think the word you want is perspicacity.

MARK: Whatever. That's the voice you're listening to.

KRISTEN: So go ahead, Donny. Let's hear your perspicacious pronouncements.

DONNY: Well...

There is a knock at the front door, it flies open and

DEEDEE bounces into the room. There is a "Hi, Deedee!" from MARK and KRISTEN but DONNY merely sniffs and takes another bite of his pizza.

DEEDEE: Cindy home?

All three shake their heads.

There's a rumour going round....

All three nod their heads.

Where is she? She blew off all her classes today.

MARK: She's lying low.

DONNY: Getting her shit together.

KRISTEN: To face Gardner.

DEEDEE: Gee! I hope she's okay.

DONNY: Gee! She's okay. She called to say she's not telling where she is but not to worry. She's at some girl-friend's place or something, s'all. And she took the cookie jar with her which was a very unfriendly gesture. Right now she's probably stoned out of her mind.

DEEDEE: And Josh?

All three point to the bedroom. DEEDEE raises her shoulders to her ears and grimaces, then whispers.

Can he hear us?

MARK: If he's got his ear to the door I imagine so.

DEEDEE: So tell me, what happened? Does anybody know?

DONNY: I do.

DEEDEE: So tell me!

DONNY takes another bite of his pizza.

DONNY: Can't. It's bad manners to talk with your mouth full.

DEEDEE: You're a brat, Donny, you know that? (*To the room in general.*) She's in real trouble, huh?

JOSH, dressed, appears from the bedroom.

JOSH: Nope, no trouble at all.

DONNY: How can you say that?!

JOSH: Very easily. You want me to say it again?

KRISTEN: You don't know what Gardner's like.

JOSH: Oh, believe me, from our brief acquaintanceship, I know exactly what the good Doctor Gardner is like.

MARK: Boy! I really don't think you do. The man is the original Eddie asshole.

JOSH: Don't you have any respect for your professors?

MARK: Sure I do. As head of the department he is totally amazing. As a human being he sucks. Cindy doesn't stand a chance.

DEEDEE: WHAT HAPPENED?

MARK: Gardner discovered the plants.

DEEDEE: NO!

DONNY: Or, rather, the plants discovered him. They fell on his head.

DEEDEE: From a windowsill? The man is short but he's not that short. (*Suspiciously.*) Or was he kneeling? I wouldn't put anything past that guy.

DONNY: He's a character out of a Molière, man.

DEEDEE: What was he doing here anyway?

KRISTEN: Evidently he offered to take a look at the computer. Something got in the works and Cindy couldn't fix it.

DEEDEE: (*To DONNY.*) You see? I knew it wasn't me when my paper went flying out there somewhere. But how did they...

JOSH: Okay, let's cut the story short. Cindy called just before he arrived and asked me to hide the plants. And I put them on the shelf in the closet.

MARK: And skeletons will fall out of closets.

KRISTEN: Among other things.

DEEDEE: Speaking purely from memory, the peeps I've had into Cindy's closet there wouldn't be room on that shelf to put a slice of mushroom from Donny's pizza, let alone half a dozen healthy flourishing marijuana plants.

DONNY: The plant is hemp. Marijuana consists of dried leaves and...

DEEDEE: Since when was botany your major?

DONNY: Since I started smoking the stuff.

JOSH: Well that's where I put them anyway. Where else was there? I couldn't put them under the bed. You know what modern divans are like. And there's only a bedside cabinet and a chest of drawers - all full. It would have been okay if the closet had stayed closed. How was I to know that's also where she keeps her software? She went to get a disc, she opened the cupboard, and the rest, as they say, is history.

DONNY: Uh-uh. The last scene is still to be played.

JOSH: Cindy will be okay. Oh, she won't be too popular with the good Doctor Gardner from here on in but, to use a phrase popular in the movies of my youth, he'll button his lip and she'll be okay. I can personally guarantee it.

They wait.

DEEDEE: Well? Are you going to tell?

JOSH: No. Sorry, Deedee. It's between me, Cindy, and the panting puritan, that's all.

DEEDEE: Okay. Donny? Kristen? We have a class in ten minutes.

KRISTEN: Yeah. (*She swings her legs off the couch and starts putting on her socks and shoes.*)

DONNY, who never removed his winter things in the previous scene and is still wearing them, takes his cap from his pocket, puts it on, picks up his backpack and mooches for the door which he opens.

DEEDEE: Hey. Wastoid! Aren't you going to wait for les girls?

DONNY stops, pulls a face, heaves a dramatic sigh, leans wearily against the doorjamb.

(*To the others.*) What's the matter with him?

DONNY: It's inhuman.

DEEDEE: What is?

DONNY: That I have to take math. Me, who can't even balance my checkbook.

MARK: Take heart, Donny, there's nobody who can.

DONNY: And what does an actor need math for anyway?

KRISTEN: (*Getting into her coat.*) To balance his checkbook. It's part of your general studies so you'd better not goof off or you'll find yourself here doing a summer session.

DONNY: Did Dustin Hoffman ever do math? Jack Nicholson? Brad Pitt?

KRISTEN: (*She has got her things.*) Ready?

MARK: Hey, Smeg, what do two and two make?

DONNY: (*Solemnly raises his middle finger.*) Get your

mother to rotate on that, asshole. (*And he goes out.*)

DEEDEE: A football player! Somebody find me a quarterback.

KRISTEN: Everybody thinks quarterbacks are so romantic. What's so special about a quarterback?

DEEDEE: At least there's the prospect of finding SOMETHING between the ears.

KRISTEN: You're SO old-fashioned. These days football players have IQ's of a hundred and seventy. They're practically geniuses.

MARK: They need to be to understand the plays.

KRISTEN: And they're very good at math.

MARK: To count up all their money.

DEEDEE: (*Shrieking.*) So find me a quarterback!

KRISTEN: (*Shoving her out of the room.*) Come on. See you guys.

MARK: Have fun.

KRISTEN: Oh, sure.

And the door closes behind them. For a moment JOSH stands smiling, then he looks down at the floor.

JOSH: Listen to that. She's still deriving some kind of comfort from the evil genius that is modern media communications.

MARK: Huh?

JOSH: The lonely old Jewish lady downstairs.

MARK: Oh... yeh... (*He goes back to his book.*)

JOSH: Does no one ever complain?

MARK: (*Shrugs.*) We never hear it. What the hell! Guess it's all part of modern living. Noise is merely another pollution.

JOSH: Are you sure she exists? Has anyone ever seen her?

MARK: I think I passed her in the lobby once. She was looking in her mailbox. It was empty.

JOSH: Not even junk mail?

MARK: Nope. Empty.

JOSH: (*Shaking his head.*) Sad... very sad...

MARK: You looking forward to going home tomorrow, Josh?

JOSH: Why do you say that?

MARK: (*Looking up from his book.*) I'm sorry we didn't give you a better time.

JOSH: It wasn't up to you to give me a good time. But thanks anyway. And, if you want to know, I have enjoyed your company.

MARK: It wasn't my company you came to enjoy.

JOSH: You were going to give me a lecture about that.

MARK: What for? You know the answers.

JOSH: Yes, I guess I do. Only I was so sure before I came. I mean... from her letters, telephone calls.

MARK: Yeah, letters and telephone calls, a good way of keeping in touch and keeping your distance. Josh, let me tell you something about my generation. May I?

JOSH: Be my guest.

MARK: Donny isn't so far off the beam when he kids about real life and the theatre being his dream world. Dream worlds seem easier. One of our professors asked his class one day how many of them came from broken homes, divorces, splits, you know. Josh, out of forty kids, about thirty put up their hands. Even they couldn't believe it when they looked around and saw how many of them there were. Then they all wanted to talk about it, tell their experiences, all at once. Man, it was like pandemonium in there. And then the tears. Kids crying in each other's arms because they'd never let the hurt out before. Happy families? Sometimes I wonder if unhappy families are maybe a better deal than no family at all. Everybody needs. And then I think of Cindy and what she's told me about her family. It wouldn't work with you and her, Josh, because my generation is a fucked-up generation that comes from a fucked-up generation. And Cindy is a good example of it. It's going to take more than sugar, daddy, to sweeten up this baby. Oh, she wasn't an abused child in the way people think of abused children, except for one uncle evidently who had an itchy finger and a mind that was a constant erection. Kinda like yours I reckon.

JOSH: Thank you.

MARK: But, so she tells me... Hey! She told you any of this?

JOSH shakes his head. Negative.

After his first attempt to jump her bones she managed to keep out of his way. It left its mark though. But what really did for her was, after her own mother got her divorce, her dad kept presenting his kids with a new mother every so many years, like he was trading in his car. To date she's had four. She gets on quite well with the latest but the problem is, she has no trust. It's hard for us to make commitments, Josh, real commitments. And it's worse for the boys. You see, boys are not supposed to cry.

JOSH nods, understanding.

She needs you as a friend, Josh. A close friend. But as a significant other? Forget it.

JOSH: You could be wrong.

MARK: I could be right.

JOSH: (*Indicating the book.*) I'm interrupting your work.

MARK: That's okay. (*He gets up and starts for the bathroom.*) I was going to take a shower anyway.

The front door opens and CINDY enters.

MARK: Oh, hi, Cindy! Where you been, girl? You okay?

CINDY nods, starts to take off her coat. MARK looks from one to the other.

I'll go take that shower.

He leaves. CINDY goes to the fridge, gets herself a soda. JOSH watches her but says nothing, waiting on her to make the first move.

CINDY: I'm sorry I walked out on you, Josh.

He gives an "It's okay but it's not really okay" kind of shrug.

I just needed to get away for a while.

JOSH: Sure.

CINDY: (*Giggles and then is serious.*) If it weren't for the fact that my whole future is on the line here it would be funny.

JOSH: Yes. Pricked pomposity is usually comical.

CINDY: (*Laughing.*) Oh, Josh! That was so pompous.

JOSH: (*Laughing with her.*) At least I'm good for a laugh if nothing else, huh?

CINDY: Shall I pack for New York?

JOSH: What? Your sense of timing is the greatest, Cindy. You know I'm due home tomorrow and classes start Monday.

CINDY:	I was kidding, Josh. What I really should have said was, what am I going to do? (*She reaches in her pocket and takes out an envelope.*) This was in my box. I have to see him in his office three o'clock tomorrow.
JOSH:	But that's when you're supposed to be taking me to the airport!
CINDY:	I've arranged for someone else to do that.
JOSH:	Seems to me, if you're in that much trouble, I mean your whole future on the line, you could have at least re-arranged your appointment with Nemesis.
CINDY:	I arranged the airport even before all this came up.
JOSH:	You what!
CINDY:	I'm sorry, I just didn't want any good-byes.
JOSH:	Good-byes?
CINDY:	Josh, the situation is obvious, isn't it?
JOSH:	Well, from what you just told me, yes, it's perfectly obvious. Oh, Cindy, I wanted to do so much for you.
CINDY:	Quit it, Josh. You wanted to do so much with me.
JOSH:	Yes.
CINDY:	And it just isn't on. As for the rest, all the things

	you wanted to do for me, thank you for thinking about it, but I don't want any of that either. I don't want to owe anybody, feel an obligation. So let's not talk about it any more. What I've got to concentrate on right this minute is tomorrow afternoon.
JOSH:	No problem.
CINDY:	What do you mean no problem? You think Gardner is just a tad ticked by this? He's a basket case! He's frothing at the mouth. One of his favourite students has turned out to be a scarlet woman, the whore of Babylon. Whatever he thinks you and I have been up to, and believe me he thinks it, is only one item in a catalogue of sins. Drugs. Alcohol.
JOSH:	No problem.
CINDY:	(*Turning away.*) Christ! (*Back.*) Add blasphemy and taking the Lord's name in vain. Can't you just feel the wrath of God about to descend on this august establishment? We'll all be pillars of salt by morning. I need a cigarette. (*She gets a pack from her coat pocket.*) My nerves can't take any more of this.
JOSH:	Cindy, okay, you don't want me to do anything for you. I accept that. But right now, right this instant I am going to do something for you. I'm going to tell you a story. What you do with it is up to you but it's something worth your knowing. Now… Doctor Gardner's father-in-law was a good ole boy from the Deep South, a judge, by the name of Langley. A man as bigoted as his son-in-law but, in the eyes of his world, a saint. That's if Protestants have saints. To the rest

of the world he was known for his racist feelings. But the good judge had some racial feelings the world didn't know about. He had, how shall I put this? A feeling for black youth. And here comes the cruncher - male youth, preferably under the age of fifteen. A good ole chicken hawk was our good ole boy. Anyway, seems like his world was on the verge of hearing all about the judge's little peccadilloes but, before it could, he suffered a hunting accident. Only it wasn't a hunting accident. It wasn't even an accident. The weapon that killed him was a handgun. Prison was never an option not for a man like Judge Langley who had sent any number there. No doubt a number of Klansmen. And how do I know all this? I heard it straight from the horse's mouth. You see, the cop who investigated the case happens to be a cousin of my wife. It's a small world. It's a funny old world. So much for this pillar of the community. It's not only televangelists and aspiring presidents who have to watch where they're pointing their peckers. (*Looking up at the ceiling.*) Funny, the wrath of God seems to have past over. I feel a distinct lightening in the gloom.

CINDY: What do you expect me to do with this amazing bit of knowledge?

JOSH: (*Shrugs.*) Whatever you want.

CINDY: But that's blackmail!

JOSH: Blackmail? Nonsense. It's a trade-off. Isn't that what life's all about? Trade-offs? Now if you were trying to use your knowledge for a little insider trading like, say, getting an A in an exam when you really deserve a D, or even an F, now that

	would be downright immoral, criminal even. And if he were to succumb to your threat then he would be acting in a criminal fashion. But, in the current circumstances, all you have to do is subtly let him know that you know and, very important this, that no one else knows, and leave the rest up to him. You haven't threatened him. Well, only obliquely.
CINDY:	And what makes you so sure he'd be worried about it anyway? It could space him out even more and then he'd really cream me.
JOSH:	Oh, he'd be worried all right. The trouble with being so self-righteous is that the slightest hint of scandal within a hundred miles of you, metaphorically speaking, and you have a bad laundry problem. When one pillar comes crashing down it can bring the whole edifice down with it. Look at Samson and the temple.
CINDY:	That was two pillars.
JOSH:	Don't be picky.
CINDY:	And what's your trade-off?
JOSH:	(*Innocently surprised.*) Mine?
CINDY:	Yes. Yours. You've just given me something. What do you want in return?
JOSH:	Oh, I've already had my trade-off.
CINDY:	How so?
JOSH:	You want to know what it is? Okay, I'll tell you. (*He pats the Buddha on the head.*) A little bit of

wisdom perhaps? Would you agree with that, ole buddy?

CINDY stands regarding JOSH for a long moment. He smiles sweetly.

CINDY: Where are we eating?

JOSH: Name it.

CINDY: I feel like gorging myself on pancakes.

JOSH: And God said, let there be pancakes, and lo there were pancakes. Oh, there's one little thing I forgot to mention.

CINDY: What's that?

JOSH: To-night you pick up the tab.

CINDY: My treat.

They both laugh. He puts his arm around her. She puts her arm around him – BLACKOUT.

In the BLACKOUT there is the SOUND of sirens, patrol cars, ambulance, and the loud klaxon of a fire wagon. The SOUND FADES and LIGHTS come up on.

SCENE SEVEN - FRIDAY AFTERNOON

The apartment appears empty. After a moment the front door opens and CINDY enters. She carries a handful of mail.

CINDY: Josh? (*She tosses the mail down on the kitchen table.*) Josh?

JOSH, dressed for going out, appears in the arch.

Ah, there you are. What you doing?

JOSH: Waiting for my lift to the airport.

CINDY: Well here she is. You all packed?

JOSH: (*Agitated.*) Cindy, I... (*Suddenly realising what she has said.*) YOU'RE taking me?

CINDY: I am. Come on, get your stuff and let's go! We'll check you in and have a nice leisurely farewell drink in the lounge.

JOSH: What happened to your date with destiny?

CINDY: Oh, I had that before lunch. I called the good doctor's secretary and I said, "Cynthia," I said, "I have this note from Doctor Gardner requesting I drop by his office at three this afternoon but I'm afraid I can't as I'm taking Professor Armstrong to the airport so can I come in and see him right now?" Well I think that rather took him by surprise because the answer came back affirmative and in I went.

JOSH: And?

CINDY: Everything's cool. Of course I had to show contrition and grovel grovel grovel, but at least I'm off the hook.

JOSH: Did you hint at your specialist knowledge of the family tree?

CINDY: The merest. I looked at the picture of Langley junior he keeps on his desk and dropped the merest hint.

JOSH: And it sufficed. I told you so.

CINDY: So you told me so. Now come on. You don't want to miss your plane do you? (*She has wandered over to the window and is now looking out and down at the street.*) Josh? Look here... there's a TV van outside... now what do you suppose?... Oh, they're interviewing someone. There's a man with a micro...

JOSH: (*Urgently waving a hand which we now see is roughly bandaged with a bloodstained handkerchief.*) Cindy! Come away from that window!

CINDY: (*Looking up and down the street.*) There's a bit of a crowd gathering. Isn't it weird how the presence of a TV camera...?

JOSH: Cindy! Come away!

CINDY: (*Turning.*) What? (*Sees his damaged hand. There is a long moment, and then.*) Oh, God, Josh! What have you been up to now?

JOSH: It's a long story.

CINDY: Shit! Does this mean I have to grovel to Gardner again?

JOSH: Not if you can get me out of here and to the airport without anyone seeing me, especially television crews.

CINDY: (*Sinking into a chair.*) Oh, my God! It's that bad?

JOSH: I've been holed up in here like a rat in a trap for the past two hours.

CINDY: Quit the dramatics, Josh. Just tell me what happened before I scream.

JOSH: (*Thoroughly alarmed.*) Don't scream! Please don't scream! That's all I need.

CINDY: Are the police after you?

JOSH: I think so, yes.

CINDY: I wondered why there were so many squad cars prowling the neighbourhood. What do they want you for?

JOSH: Breaking and entering, attempted burglary, aggravated assault, attempted rape. I don't know. You name it they'll throw it at me.

CINDY stares at him, speechless and open-mouthed.

It all started with Ravel.

CINDY: Ravel? Ravel who? Who's Ravel?

JOSH: Ravel the composer.

CINDY: Ravel? He's dead! Isn't he? He's been dead for years. And he's not even American.

JOSH: I was listening to the radio, I finally tracked down the classical station by the way, one of my favourite pieces, "Pavanne For A Dead Princess," do you know it?

CINDY growls and claws the air.

>Beautiful... One of Ravel's most sublime melodies...

CINDY: Is this ridiculous or is this ridiculous? Josh, I am going to scream. I feel a scream coming on.

JOSH: No! Wait! Suddenly, from downstairs, Mrs Lasker's goddam television again.

CINDY: Mrs Who?

JOSH: Lasker! Lasker! You see? You don't even know her name! It's on her mailbox!

CINDY: I don't go around reading people's names on mailboxes! (*Raising her hands, placating.*) Okay, Josh, okay. Just calm down and tell me...

JOSH: So I went downstairs intending to ask her, very nicely of course, to turn down the volume. I knocked. No answer. I knocked again. I waited. I banged! Three other doors opened. Hers didn't. So I went outside and round to her window and looked in. There was the television, There was old Mrs Lasker. But she looked... sort of strange.

CINDY: Strange?

JOSH: I thought maybe she was dead, or in a coma or something. Well, you hear these stories don't you? About people dying and being found days, even weeks, after and... but this is the point...

CINDY: We're getting to a point?

JOSH: There was this old fashioned electric heater and I could see smoke coming from it. So then I thought she's been overcome by the smoke. So I broke the window, Climbed in, got across the room and yanked the plug out of the receptacle, which meant I had my back to her. The next thing I knew, this virago, this Amazon, this wild woman, this harridan from hell whose life I was trying to save was beating me to death with a hockey stick! I was being mugged by an athletic geriatric!

CINDY: Didn't you try to explain? Didn't you defend yourself?

JOSH: Hey! She was screaming like a banshee. And a hockey stick in the hands of a ninety year old game show TV addict weighing in at eighty pounds is a deadly weapon.

CINDY: So what did you do?

JOSH: I did what any sane person would do, I fled. (*He groans and rubs a bruised shoulder.*) I was out of the door so fast I could have broken an Olympic record. This time of course, lucky for me, none of the neighbours opened their doors. When the shit hits the fan keep your noses out of it. I hightailed it back up here. She couldn't have seen me. Must've thought I ran off down the street.

CINDY: What happened about the fire?

JOSH: How do I know? She probably pissed on it till the firemen got here. And the cops weren't long after, and the ambulance. And if I was to get someone like Judge Langley trying my case I'd

	go down for a hundred years.
CINDY:	Do you think she'll be able to recognise you?
JOSH:	After all the cop series she's watched? You betcha. Anyone would. If nothing else, this is... (*He indicates his black eye.*) ... And this... (*The bandaged hand.*) She'll have given the cops a full description. Now how are we going to get me to the airport, Cindy? I've got a plane to catch.
CINDY:	Poor old Josh. You could have been a hero, saving an old lady's life, and, instead, you're a fugitive. It's a bit like a TV script isn't it?
JOSH:	I didn't do it to be a hero, Cindy. I've no wish to be a hero. But she'll have her moment of glory now. I can just see the headlines. "Superannuated super Grannie annihilates would-be assailant." She won't be watching TV, she'll be on it. Which only goes to prove anyone CAN be famous for that fifteen minutes. I tell you, if I ever get out of this, it'll be one spring break I'll never forget. I couldn't have been in more peril if I'd gone to South America and mixed it with a drugs cartel.
CINDY:	Josh, why don't you just call the police and tell them what really happened?
JOSH:	Are you out of your mind?
CINDY:	But then you'd be in the clear.
JOSH:	In the first place it's her word against mine and why should they want to believe me?
CINDY:	You're a respectable university lecturer.

JOSH: Judge Langley was a highly respectable judge and look what happened to him. And who's going to be a character witness? Doc Gardner? I can just see him in court when he takes the stand, gloating oh so smugly, so self-righteous. And, in the second place, Cindy, I am trying to avoid any kind of publicity.

CINDY: Exposure.

JOSH: That too. And catch my plane home.

CINDY: (*Looking at her watch.*) Okay, we might have lost out on that nice leisurely drink but we've still got time. Let's see... dark glasses!

JOSH: It's winter, Cindy and getting dark. I want to avoid attention, not attract it.

CINDY: All right then, a little judicious make-up will disguise the black eye. And a band-aid on the hand over which you can slip your glove. Wait here. (*She pushes him down into a chair and starts for the bathroom, comes back.*) Oh, I nearly forgot, there's a letter for you.

JOSH: For me?

She finds the letter on the table, hands it to him, and goes. JOSH opens the letter and reads. CINDY returns with the make-up which she puts on the table.

CINDY: Okay.

She sees JOSH staring straight ahead.

Josh? What's the matter? Bad news?

JOSH: (*Looks at the letter, looks up at her.*) It's from Rita.

CINDY: Your wife? What does she say?

JOSH: (*Shrugs.*) Nothing much. She wants a divorce.

He hands CINDY the letter. She reads.

CINDY: Oh, Josh. I am sorry. Do you know the guy?

JOSH: Sure. He's one of my students. One of my favourite students. (*He takes back the letter and looks at it.*) Sounds like sauce for the goose wouldn't you say? (*He turns back to her and points to his eye.*) Hey! (*She starts on the make-up. After a moment.*) You want to know something?

CINDY: What?

JOSH: This is cosy. (*Pause.*) What say we go somewhere and have a nice leisurely drink? (*Pause.*) And what say we then call the airport and book two seats for the big A?

CINDY smiles and shrugs. JOSH turns and looks at the Buddha, looks out front.

Because, if we ever get out of this alive, the rest, as they say, is history.

She carries on making up his eye. He puts his arm around her waist. His hand is still bandaged.

www.ingramcontent.com/pod-product-compliance
Lightning Source LLC
Chambersburg PA
CBHW020008050426
42450CB00005B/361